regarding
animals

In the series
Animals, Culture, and Society

edited by Clinton R. Sanders and Arnold Arluke

regarding animals

Arnold Arluke & Clinton R. Sanders

Temple University Press
Philadelphia

Temple University Press, Philadelphia 19122
Copyright © 1996 by Temple University. All rights reserved
Published in 1996
Printed in the United States of America

Text design by Chiquita Babb

Library of Congress Cataloging-in-Publication Data
Arluke, Arnold.
    Regarding animals / Arnold Arluke and Clinton R. Sanders.
      p.   cm. — (Animals, culture, and society)
    Includes bibliographical references and index.
    ISBN 1-56639-440-6 (cloth : alk. paper). — ISBN 1-56639-441-4
(paper : alk. paper)
    1. Human–animal relationships.   2. Animals—Social aspects.   I. Sanders,
Clinton.   II. Title.   III. Series.
QL85.A75   1996
304.2'7—dc20   95-43062

ISBN 13: 978-1-56639-441-3 (paper : alk. paper)

052008

contents

acknowledgments

We have been fortunate to have been able to draw on the help and advice of many colleagues and friends. Eileen Crist, Elizabeth Lawrence, and James Serpell provided critical comments on the entire book. Hal Herzog, Alan Klein, Jack Levin, Eleanor Lyon, Lauren Rolfe, Andrew Rowan, and Earl Rubington offered guidance and support at various stages of the project. Jason Miranda used computer skills to enhance the cover photo.

We also would like to thank publishers for permission to use some of our prior work. Chapter 2 is an expanded and revised version of a paper entitled "If Lions Could Speak: Investigating the Animal–Human Relationship and the Perspectives of Nonhuman Others" that was first published in *Sociological Quarterly* 34:377–390, 1993 (©1993 by Midwest Sociology Society. Reprinted by permission). Chapter 4 appeared as "Managing Emotions in an Animal Shelter" in *Animals and Human Society* (London: Routledge, 1994), 145–65, edited by Aubrey Manning and James Serpell. Chapter 6 was originally co-authored with Boria Sax as "Understanding Nazi Animal Protection and the Holocaust" in *Anthrozoös* 5(1992):6–31, and as "The Nazi Treatment of Animals and People" in *Reinventing Biology* (Bloomington: Indiana University Press, 1995), 228–60, edited by Lynda Birke and Ruth Hubbard.

Funding for the research in Chapters 3 and 4 came from the William and Charlotte Parks Trust. Funding was also provided by the Research and Scholarship Fund of Northeastern University.

regarding animals

introduction

Bringing Animals to the Center

THE COMMANDING PRESENCE of nonhuman animals in our society is largely taken for granted. Most of us have observed that even the harshest people completely change their demeanor when speaking of a cherished companion animal, but we generally explain the inconsistency as a personal quirk. So information that gives some rough measure of our investment in animals is rather startling. What does it mean that zoos draw far more people than professional sporting events (Maple 1995) or that pet owners spend more on animal food than parents spend on baby food (Albert and Bulcroft 1987) or that by the 1980s the U.S. Congress was receiving more letters about animal welfare than any other issue (Fox 1990)? In a time of sensitivity to how language shapes attitudes, one frequently hears people characterize others with animal images; think of the positive associations connected with calling someone a pussycat or teddy bear, or the negative (sometimes racist) ones that arise in calling someone a rat or a gorilla or a snake. But what do such associations say about the animals? If animals have such a strong hold on our minds and hearts, what accounts for social scientists' lack of intellectual engagement with the meaning and uses of animals in modern life?

Although there is an enormous literature about animals by novelists, journalists, philosophers, biologists, psychologists, and animal behaviorists, we have been disappointed that there is so little by our fellow sociologists. The more we study animals, the more fertile the field seems to be for further sociological exploration. The lack of interest seems to be due largely to sociology's belief that relationships (which require self-consciousness and understanding of others) depend on verbal facility and the use of language. But also playing a part in this reticence is the false belief that animals occupy a far less important place in advanced industrial societies than they do in nonindustrial ones.

Although Clifton Bryant has criticized his colleagues in sociology for having "often been myopic" and disregarding "the permeating social influence of animals in our larger cultural fabric and our more idiosyncratic individual modes of interaction and relationships," his advocacy of a "zoological focus" has generated little response (Bryant 1979, 400). Most sociological research is anthropocentric (or human-centered) and focuses on relationships among humans (for exceptions, see Cohen 1989; Latour 1988; Turkle 1984).

In research on settings where animals are major actors, they are still not brought to center stage even though they figure prominently in the thinking and feeling of the people being studied. Look at a recent article on game wardens (Palmer 1985); this fine study of the problems and techniques of being an environmental "police officer" will disappoint readers interested in what game wardens think about the animals they protect and the kinds of interactions and relationships they form with them "on the job." In a variety of settings in which animals are of central importance—from bird watching (Donnelly 1994) to fishing (Miller and Van Maanen 1982), social scientists train their gaze exclusively on people and seem uninterested in how people interact with and give meaning to the animals themselves.

Anthropological research is a notable exception. Mary Douglas (1966), E. E. Evans-Pritchard (1956), Edmund Leach (1964), and Claude Lévi-Strauss (1966) first observed that animals serve as useful instruments of culture because they are highly flexible symbols. Others have followed their lead; in fact, it has become a "thriving field" in anthropology (Shanklin 1985, 379) to study animals as a window into human thinking and needs (cf., Ingold 1988; Tambiah 1969: Willis 1974, 1990).

Take the case of cockfighting. To the anthropologist Clifford Geertz (1972), the Balinese people understand the cockfight as more than a bloody battle of "a chicken hacking another mindlessly to bits." Just under the surface of the cockfight, a more symbolic action is occurring. Owners' personalities are "mirrored" in their birds because they so deeply identify with them, just as American cock owners have been found to express their masculinity through the fighting prowess of their animals (Hawley 1993). Beyond the cockfight itself, Geertz claims, is the understanding of the animals as metaphors of larger Balinese culture; the cockfight becomes a story the Balinese tell themselves about how their society is structured and what the structure means to them. The bird is so tied into their national self-perception that the Balinese even describe the physical shape of their island as a proud cock. What they see in the fight is a "status bloodbath" that "displays" deep concerns about human relationships in Balinese society that are unmentionable in everyday life.

Despite anthropologists' interest in animals, their work is limited because it addresses mainly traditional societies. There is every reason to think that animals play an equally important symbolic role in the lives of people in industrialized societies as they do in Bali. The intellectual mandate of sociology—to understand the relationship between private experience and the wider society—positions it perfectly to examine this role.

The timing for undertaking such a study is also ideal. Contemporary sociological ethnography, or the description of a group's way of life, is moving beyond the study and representation of the traditional, clearly defined "other" and into more diverse and novel milieus. Because nonhuman outsiders are removed from most researchers not by class or ethnicity but by biology, research on human exchanges with animals breaks new academic ground. But it is also rooted in traditional sociological ethnography. Exploring the human-animal relationship is similar to the perspective of the work of the University of Chicago fieldworkers who, in the 1920s and 1930s, studied groups outside the bounds of middle-class society—gang members, hoboes, dance hall girls, and other unfamiliar groups. Our project is similarly unconventional and no less exciting.

For practical and scholarly reasons, we believe that undertaking this work is important. As concern mounts and consciousness changes—about, for example, managing wildlife populations or conducting scientific experiments—research will contribute to the reasoned and informed arguments in what are often emotionally charged and highly polarized debates over public policies regarding animals. Studying animals and human interactions with them enables us to learn about ourselves as social creatures. It will show us, among other things, how meaning is socially created in interaction, even with nonhumans; how we organize our social world; and how we see our connection (or lack of it) to other living things. It may even reveal our most essential conceptions of social order and our most authentic attitudes toward people.

This book, then, is not about animals per se but about how humans regard them in modern Western societies. When we look at these attitudes, one of the most glaring consistencies is inconsistency, or what Andrew Rowan (Herzog 1993, 349) calls the "constant paradox." Veterinary students become upset when they "sacrifice" certain mice, but not others (Herzog et al. 1989). A nursing student reports that she enjoys dissecting dogs in biology class but could never dissect her own pet. A woman decides to have her adored pet dog killed like an "animal" after it bites her sister (Hickrod and Schmitt 1982). At one moment hunting dogs are the subject of proud boasting because they have keen tracking abilities; at the next they are kicked hard enough to crack their ribs because they have gotten in the way (Jordan 1975). A journalist is repulsed by the carnage he witnesses in a Midwestern slaughterhouse but later finds his own experience of firing a steel bolt into the head of a steer to be "as easy as hitting pop flies to the outfield" (Lesy 1987). Three teenaged boys lure a dog onto the railroad tracks as a horrified young girl watches an oncoming train crush the animal. Although the judge in this case receives thousands of letters from angry citizens venting their rage at these boys, he gets no such expressions of outrage when a black boy is savagely beaten and killed by a gang of white youths (Cullen 1992).

Inconsistent behavior toward animals is omnipresent in Western society. Rather than adding to a litany of examples or decrying its moral and emotional consequences, we want to understand it sociologically. From the sociologist's perspective, what is most interesting is not to identify such contradictions or reveal the assumptions underlying them—a task more ably served by philosophers—but to understand better what it is about modern society that makes it possible for people to shower animals with affection and to maltreat or kill them, to regard them as sentient creatures and also as utilitarian objects. How is it that people seem able to balance such significantly conflicting values and live comfortably with such contradiction? How is it that instead of examining these conflicts, so few people are even aware of them?

We take this ordinary ambivalence toward animals as a sign that social forces must be working successfully, so successfully that in modern societies many people do not experience these contradictions as a problem. As sociologists, our task is to identify some of the key social forces behind the capricious treatment of animals and show how they operate. Our large goal, though, is to make a plea for the value of sociological analysis in popular and academic discussions of animals in contemporary Western life. How we undertake such analysis is the subject of the first chapter.

the human-animal tribe

chapter 1

The Human Point of View

The essential vocation of interpretive anthropology is not to answer
our deepest questions, but to make available to us answers that others, guarding other sheep in other valleys, have given, and thus to
include them in the consultable record of what man has said.

—Clifford Geertz, *The Interpretation of Cultures*

SYMBOLIC INTERACTIONISTS have long argued that all meaning
is a product of social interaction rather than a quality inherent in the
objects themselves. Although animals have a physical being, once in
contact with humans, they are given a cultural identity as people try
to make sense of them, understand them, use them, or communicate
with them. They are brought into civilization and transformed accordingly as their meaning is socially constructed. To say that animals are social constructions means that we have to look beyond
what is regarded as innate in animals—beyond their physical appearance, observable behavior, and cognitive abilities—in order to
understand how humans will think about and interact with them.
"Being" an animal in modern societies may be less a matter of biology than it is an issue of human culture and consciousness.

9

Animals as Social Constructions

As social constructions, the meanings of animals seem to be fixed and enduring. The tenacious persistence and widespread acceptance of these meanings suggest that they are cultural phenomena—part of the normative order of the society in which they occur. Much like other cultural phenomena—love of country, motherhood, or the success ethic—the meanings of animals are passed from generation to generation.

Consider which animals are regarded as wild, and which as tame. At an early age, we learn by watching Disney movies, reading fairy tales, and listening to our parents that a "wild animal" can be a tiger in the jungle, an elephant in a zoo, a squirrel living in the backyard of a suburban home, an ownerless dog that roams the neighborhood, or a mean-spirited, raunchy person looking to pick a fight in a bar. As social designations, "wildness" comes to mean distance and danger with "tameness" its converse. Many learn what a "tame" animal is by owning one themselves. Parents often acquire pets for their children who themselves in turn attribute personlike qualities to these animals and protect them from the dangers that lurk outside in the world of nature. The result is that children come to view what constitutes a wild or tame animal as a hard and fast "fact" whose meaning is a given—external to human culture and social process. Yet we know sociologically that "facts" can vary because in different places and times people will assign them different meanings.

Place and Time

In contemporary American homes, for example, it is taken for granted that dogs will be regarded in a certain way. Lucy Hickrod and Raymond Schmitt (1982) have described the process by which a puppy is transformed from a novelty or toy into a make-believe or "pretend" family member that is named, fed, groomed, dressed, photographed, talked to, mourned, slept with, given birthday parties, and taken to "therapists" for behavior problems. This process

The Human–Animal Tribe

begins when a dog is taken into a home. Given the high value placed on pets in America, at this stage people are encouraged to accept the pet into their families. Naming the new pet begins its transformation from a generic puppy into a specific member of the family. The name affords the dog an identity and makes it easier to talk about and direct activities toward it as though it were part of the family. Acquiring a status in the family is contingent on family members' willingness to meet the pet's needs. Pets that do not obey "house rules" or that are considered "too difficult" may be given away or euthanized. If pets survive this probationary period, many family members develop intense feelings about them. During this "engrossment stage," personal qualities such as loyalty or humorousness are often attributed to pets, who are seen as being more consistent in displaying these attributes than are most humans.

After becoming engrossed in their dogs, most owners come to the realization that they are treating their pets as genuine family members. As they became aware of their feelings for their animals, owners often are amazed at how intensely family members care about the pets even though they are "only animals." Soon they begin to communicate their feelings for their pets to people outside the family so they too can participate in this definition of the animal as family member. This may entail introducing pets to newcomers by mentioning their names and discussing their personal histories, as well as nonverbally communicating this status through fondling, special dressing, or the like. These "tie signs" minimize the social boundaries between pets and humans, thereby demonstrating their special position to strangers.

Even after pets die, their intimate connection to families may be remembered when stories are shared about the animals' exploits or when later pets are given the same names. Since human emotional response to the death of a pet can be as intense as those precipitated by the loss of any family member (Carmack 1985; Cowles 1985), it is not surprising that there is a modest but growing interest in burying pets in animal cemeteries in order to maintain this connection (Cooke 1988). That dead animals are typically treated as kin can be seen in the intense public disapproval generated by media reports that Roy Rogers stuffed his faithful steed Trigger so that it could be displayed in Rogers' living room. This negative reaction, no doubt, arose because the public regarded the horse as a pet or member of the Rodgers family. Presumably, for these people the stuffing of a pet, rather than a hunting trophy, seemed to deny an emotional tie by turning Trigger into an object.

However, Hickrod and Schmitt (1982), claim that a pet is still something less than a family member because of ever present "frame breaks." Bystanders, media presentations, and certain situations constantly call into question this definition of the pet as a family member and reinforce its definition as an animal or a toy. Signs reading "No Pets Allowed" or "Beware of Guard Dog," as well as instances when pets nonchalantly vomit in living rooms, eat their own excrement, or mate in public are reminders that they are, at best, make-believe members of families.

Yet dogs in another setting might be anything but adjunct members of the family. In the context of a dog track, they are racing machines (Cantwell 1993). This construction requires impersonal identities, and the dogs are assigned special names and numbers. Their official names appear in the programs but are almost never used, except when announced with their position numbers at the checkpoint. These official names, like the names of race horses, exist outside everyday human usage, and their meanings are clear only to those deeply involved in the race world. These names are not even anthropomorphized, but usually refer to abstract images or emotional states—such as Peaceful Darkness, Fine Style, or Surprise Launch. When names are humanized, they are almost always in the possessive form, such as Tara's Dream or Bob's Showtime, suggesting that the names apply to the owners and not the dogs. Transforming the dogs into machines reduces their identities to numbers that appear on racing blankets, starting gates, programs, handlers' armbands, and monitors displaying betting odds. The numbers are also used by track announcers when dogs pass through the checkpoint and during the race to indicate their position as well as by bettors who shout numbers, not names, as they cheer on their choices.

Standard handling practice also helps to construct a numbered machine, suppressing the dogs' personalities. For example, when the dogs are presented to interested bettors in the paddock, steel bars keep onlookers about five feet from the thick glass behind which the dogs, handlers, and judges do their work. The distance and the glass muffle all sounds, although one can still hear the barking of unmuzzled dogs in cages turned away from the public's view. When in view, they are muzzled and tightly controlled. Muzzling partially covers their faces, restricts their barking, and gives them a badge of human dominance. Handlers rarely look at, talk to, or touch their dogs, and the exceptions only point to the more pervasive construction of these animals as machines. Occasionally, when handlers talk to each other, they might quickly pet or scratch a dog's head or neck. This touching looks more like a reflex or afterthought, because they neither look nor talk to the dog as they do it, nor do they try to solicit any response from the dog. For the most part, the dogs themselves make little response. No dog, for instance, responds by licking a handler's hand or jumping up on the handler. Indeed, the greyhounds rarely initiate any interaction with each other: they are trained not to do so, and the handlers will stop any attempt. For example, after one dog's muzzle was removed, it started licking the face of the adjacent dog. Showing a barely detectable smile, the handler instantly used the leash to pull the licking dog away.

At these rare times when people try to interact with the greyhounds, the handlers immediately restrain the dogs and ignore the people, almost as though nothing had happened. In one instance, two young boys broke through the wooden barrier separating the public from the dogs being led from the paddock to the track. The dogs looked startled but as they started to respond and turn toward the boys, the handlers instantly shortened the leashes on the dogs, pulled them forward, and pushed the boys outside the barrier, never losing a step in the process. Even when the dogs and the handlers were not busy, such interactions were prevented. One bettor, for instance, stood very close to the paddock's glass while the dogs were in line to be weighed. She caught one dog's eye and suddenly reached out as if to pet it, putting her hand on the glass inches away from the head of the muzzled dog. With that, the dog became visibly excited, turned around and looked at her. As soon as its muzzle hit the glass, it was abruptly pulled closer to the handler and farther away from the spectator.

The meaning of social constructions can change over time. What a group regards as wild can at another time be regarded as tame. For example, our conception of primates has developed dramatically in the twentieth century, so that their place in the modern order has changed from being exotic and wild to being tame and almost human. Anthropologist Susan Sperling (1988) claims that several factors account for this shifting view. As postwar America grew increasingly interested in the complex cognitive and social abilities of animals, images of primates in particular were remodeled to become more humanlike. Anthropological models of evolution started replacing "primitive" human groups, such as the Trobriand Islanders, with nonhuman primates—making the latter our "ancestors." These models along with observational studies of primates were disseminated to the public in magazines like *National Geographic*, nature shows on television, or in movies like *Gorillas in the Mist*, giving the impression of extreme similarity between the species. Baboon troops, for instance, were uncritically viewed as microcosms of human society because they too had social characteristics, such as a "division of labor." Compounding the effect of this research were field studies, like those of Jane Goodall's, in which chimpanzee subjects were given human names and their personalities described in human terms. Additional anthropomorphization came from researchers who studied the acquisition of language by apes and treated their animals like foster children who could talk and live in human settings. The consequence, contends Sperling (1988), was the "obliteration" of the border between humans and nonhumans.

With such boundary blurring, it is not surprising that what were once wild animals may now be regarded as pets. A case in point is a project that allowed laypeople to assist with research and conservation efforts with wild orangutans in Borneo (Russell 1995). Some people had expected and desired to have a "cuddly" experience with these animals and, not surprisingly, experienced the apes as "children" in their interactions with confiscated infants, which were to be sold as pets but were being rehabilitated in a clinic. Although they were initially forbidden to have physical contact with the infants, many of the tourists expressed an intense desire to hold them. Russell reports that many "oohed" and "aahed" when seeing the animals and commonly described them as "cute" or as "sweet little ones." When permitted physical contact, all the tourists felt very fortunate to have the opportunity, saying that it "profoundly" affected them. Some tourists even competed for the affections of certain infants, as they sought to "babysit" them or were reluctant to break off contact because they felt "needed" by the young animals. No longer seen as alien or strange creatures as they might have been years ago, these primates were related to in the only way that made sense to these tourists. They defined the primates as pets or as quasi-family members of human society.

In fact, some wild animals are literally transformed over time into pets, of a sort. Elizabeth Lawrence (1990) contends that this century has witnessed "a remarkable American social phenomenon" in the transformation of wild bears into tame and civilized stuffed teddy bear dolls that hardly resemble their natural forebears. Although the teddy bear is obviously an inanimate object, a doll, it is now often seen and treated as though it were a pet or "companion animal." Indeed, Lawrence goes so far as to say that "teddy bears are animals that nearly, but not quite, become people" (p. 151). Child and adult owners attribute personalities, thoughts, feelings, and behaviors to their teddy bears and, not surprisingly, report that their dolls make them feel comfortable. In return for the "spirit of caring and unconditional affection" provided by the dolls, owners cherish them (p. 152). This conversion of nature into culture, according to Lawrence, has resulted in a "counterpart of oppositions" between the teddy bear and the living bear. The former is "tame, dependent, dependable, neutered, civilized, humanized and sanitized," while the latter is "wild, unpredictable, uncontrolled, aloof," and dangerous (p. 150). Lawrence's analysis highlights the power of social constructions to alter what we think of as normal or natural—they do nothing less than shape our consciousness.

Normal and Natural

What are animals in zoos, for instance? They are animals that most of us will never see in their "natural" state, but can only read about or imagine. Taken from their "natural" context, these animals are put in a human frame while their natural habitat is transformed into our dream of a human–animal paradise (Sax n.d.). They become creatures of leisure—given food rather than hunting and fighting for live game among themselves. Even the "prey" is transformed so that it cannot be identified as a specific animal—meat is thoroughly butchered—and zoo animals are not allowed to eat fellow captives. Zoo animals also live in harmony, never struggling over territorial matters with other animals. They live in an environment built by humans: a constructed world that shrinks entire continents into acres and often combines different species in the same exhibit, even though they may live far apart in their normal climatic zone.

The artificiality of this zoological paradise, as Boria Sax (n.d.) perceptively observes, renders the traditional dichotomy of wild versus domestic animals invalid. There, symbols of captivity such as cages and cold cement floors increasingly are being eliminated, while animals in nature are being carefully observed and controlled through devices such as concealed cameras and radio collars. Because of modes of modern captivity, animals can be closely approached and admired in ways that are impossible in the wild. This proximity means that humans are not unobtrusive to zoo animals. Although it is not known exactly how their behavior changes, one study (Hosey and Druck 1987) found that, instead of ignoring or being habituated to visitors, zoo animals respond to and interact with them. In a study of captive bears (Forthman et al. 1992), for instance, these animals frequently

The Human–Animal Tribe

demonstrated stereotypic locomotor patterns and were often encouraged by the public to beg. What zoo visitors see, then, is a culturally falsified version of how these animals actually behave in the "wild."

The result is often a captive wild animal that is regarded as a human in animal skin. Perhaps one of the best examples of this transformation is the giant panda. Many of the panda's physical features—the round head, large eyes, and vertical posture—facilitate its anthropomorphization. The panda is not a distant animal but becomes a cuddly friend "imbued with a human personality, with human needs, and subject to similar emotions" (Mullan and Marvin 1987, xiv-xv). Once perceived in this manner, the distinction crumbles between what we regard as wild and tame. Thus, visitors often have a fondness for zoo animals, sometimes naming them, "adopting" them, giving them tea parties, or playing with and touching them in children's zoos and aquaria petting tanks. For their part, animal handlers often form even closer relationships with individual zoo animals, treating them as typical companion animals.

If social constructions can tinker with actors' consciousness of the "natural" order, they can just as easily toy with other basic distinctions that humans make including those between life and death. An example of this is the taxidermist who tries to make dead animals appear animated or "just as they were in life" (Bryant and Shoemaker 1988). Unlike those in real life or even the zoo, however, the stuffed wild animal can be examined closely and handled without fear. Some of these transformations into inanimate life are intended to be instructional, as in the case of museums that display animals faithful to their "natural state" in order to teach the public or stimulate interest in zoology. Other transformations symbolize human domination over nature as hunters do who display their trophy animals on walls or on floors. In contrast to the hunter's trophy, some pet owners stuff and display a deceased animal as a memorial to its faithful companionship. This practice was common—though the source of some controversy—among middle-class Parisian dog owners during the nineteenth century (Kete 1993).

Stuffed animals or animal skins may also be used as product trademarks, home decoration, or fashion statements to project certain images and capture attention. When used as fashion statements, they can, to some degree, transform their owners' personae. Fur coats for women, for instance, in addition to being used as status symbols suggesting affluence, can offer a reflection of animal spirit or passion by projecting an exotic or erotic image, while leather coats on men can convey a macho attitude. In this way, the distinction between wild and tame becomes sufficiently blurred to allow some humans to entertain the idea that they are a little "wild."

In some instances, humans may transform the "natural" order by reshaping the very disposition and biology of animals. For example, over centuries, the English bulldog was bred to be a one-hundred-pound, muscular fighter with a deep chest, powerful jaw, and a setback nose for the sport of bullbaiting. Breeders were unconcerned with beauty while giving special attention to such traits as savagery and insensitivity to pain. Despite the eventual outlawing of bullbaiting and bulldogs, dog lovers resisted the edicts and used selective breeding methods to preserve all the bulldog's traits except its ferocity. The result over a few generations was the exaggerated appearance and pleasant personality of the modern English bulldog (Nash 1989). What the human consciousness takes for granted as innate biology is, at least in the case of the bulldog, the result of decades of social (and genetic) construction.

Studying Constructs

In this way, then, people operating in the "real world" produce a construction of reality that influences their behavior toward animals. The method known in social science as ethnography, or fieldwork, is uniquely suited to studying the process by which people construct these meanings. We fieldworkers discover these meanings by immersing ourselves in unfamiliar worlds, or what anthropologists think of as the "exotic bush." Whether we are looking at cockfighting in the barrios of San Juan or dog walking on the streets of New York, we participate face-to-face with people in their natural settings and share in their activities (Bruyn 1966). For ethnographers of human–animal relationships, our exotic tribes are pet owners, veterinarians, animal trainers, slaughterhouse workers, mounted policemen, and any other group that works with or cares for animals, and our "bush" is the pet store, circus, riding stable, and countless other settings where animals play a part.

For Arluke, this has often meant venturing into milieus where animals are killed, such as animal shelters, research labs, and medical schools, while Sanders has frequented places where animals are cared for, such as veterinary clinics and dog training schools. As ethnographers, we have both sought to document what is happening in these unfamiliar places and to unearth the meanings that animals have for people. This work involves taking an unsentimental look at what the world is like backstage to people who have learned to see, hear, speak, think, and act in ways that may be very different from our own. To do this may mean learning a new language, or argot, watching and participating in activities, and talking with countless "natives."

The fieldworker's most fundamental role, then, is that of a student who learns how other people see and experience the world, or what some call the "native's point of view" (Geertz 1974). One learns by taking a phenomenological approach in the field—that is, considering what people say and do as a product of how they interpret the meaning of events, objects, and situations. For the ethnographer, meaning—including how animals are defined—is negotiable, changing, and context-dependent. The goal of the fieldworker is to document this process of interpretation through empathic understanding (or *verstehen*), reproducing in his or her mind, and experiencing firsthand, the feelings, motives, and thoughts behind the actions of others. In short, the fieldworker tries to grasp the meanings of the subjects' behavior by seeing things from their point of view.

Into the Field

Fieldwork begins long before researchers enter their chosen worlds. The selection of a general problem to study may come from reviewing the literature, but it will be heavily influenced by the prior sociological training of researchers and their personal experiences (Burgess 1984). What led us to study human–animal relationships? For over ten years, Arluke's work largely focused on understanding the behavior of patients and health-care providers. His sociological skills made him quite comfortable in medical settings where he could speak the argot of medicine and follow the folkways of this social world. While at work on a study of the folklore of arthritis patients, some of the physicians with whom Arluke collaborated led him unknowingly into a dog laboratory as he trailed along with them, ostensibly to learn more about arthritis. As the physicians spoke with a colleague in this lab, Arluke noticed a lack of interaction between a lab dog and two technicians. He was struck by the seeming indifference of the technicians to the dog's solicitations over several minutes. It was almost as though the dog did not exist for them, he thought, as they started to set up some equipment needed for an experiment. As he left the lab with the physicians, one turned to him and muttered, "I don't want to be in here when they start the experiment." Arluke wondered how the technicians could ignore the dog and perform the experiment while the physician couldn't wait to leave? What was it about the immediate social scene of the lab that made it possible for workers to experiment on animals? This was one of many early questions that drew Arluke into this research area and, over the following years, into other aspects of the human–animal relationship.

Following the death of his long-time canine companion in 1988, Sanders acquired two Newfoundland puppies. Although he had, for some time, planned to investigate the unique relationship that develops between blind people and their dogs, his first foray into this specialized world of interaction convinced him that he needed a foundation of knowledge about the general process by which people develop relationships with companion animals. Unavoidably, as he was spending massive amounts of time with his new companions, Sanders decided to examine systematically the interactional process in which he was deeply involved. In the fall of 1988, Sanders, the

Newfoundland puppies, and his partner enrolled in an eight-week "puppy kindergarten" class, which met in a local veterinary clinic and was led by an academically trained animal behaviorist. The class included some ten dogs (ranging in age from twelve to fifteen weeks) and their owners. The purpose of the training was basic socialization—to accustom the animals to other dogs and humans and teach the owners elementary techniques for developing satisfactory relationships with their pets. As a direct participant, Sanders became interested in how the people in the class attributed motives to their puppies or excused their misbehavior or mistakes. He began to record his observations of the interactions within the class after each two-hour session ended. The next spring, with permission of the trainer, Sanders attended another class sequence and, from an unobtrusive location, systematically recorded fieldnotes detailing the interactions and activities observed. The puppy classes provided an excellent opportunity to see aspects of this developmental process in action.

Having established this basic grounded understanding of the canine–human relationship, Sanders then approached the administrators of the veterinary hospital and received permission to observe clinical interactions among the doctors, owner–clients, and animal–patients. During the next twelve months of participant observation, Sanders collected additional information on animal–human exchanges. He also developed an interest in the day-to-day occupational experience of veterinarians, which increasingly became the focus of his research.

Before entering certain settings, researchers must often obtain permission from insiders. While certain arenas of activity are public and therefore within the ethical purview of researchers to observe, talk, and participate without revealing their identity, many are not. Since it is rare for ethnographers to be invited into private settings, entering these locations often involves jumping a number of hurdles ranging from negotiations with powerful formal figures, or "gatekeepers," to endless meetings and written statements explaining who fieldworkers are and what they want. In exchange for being allowed to observe, ethnographers usually strike a research bargain promising confidentiality and no interference with activities (Bogdan and Taylor 1975).

Often this process of entrée involves trickling down the formal hierarchy of power and authority. This was typically the case in most of the laboratories Arluke studied, not only because these labs were usually part of a larger and more complex organization such as a hospital or a university, but because the research community has become increasingly suspicious of the motives of outsiders who may want to sabotage animal experimentation, hurt experimenters, or write tabloid exposés of cruelty to animals. For these reasons, the obstacles to getting into a lab seemed daunting to Arluke, and he almost abandoned the project. One after another, he met with a succession of gatekeepers—a hospital vice president, the head of the animal care committee, the director of public relations, the head of one of the medical departments, the chief technician of one of its labs, and lastly the lab's technicians and caretakers. It took him over three months to get permission to study his first lab.

Working in somewhat smaller, less bureaucratized situations, settings where there was little fear of an exposé, Sanders faced fewer obstacles. In both the veterinary clinic and the guide-dog training program, he was "sponsored" by members whom he already knew. At the veterinary hospital he was introduced and "taught the ropes" by a clinic partner he had known for more than a decade. Similarly, in the dog training program, Sanders was introduced to the staff and the setting by a trainer who had been enrolled in one of his university classes some years before.

Participant Observation

As fieldwork gets under way, ethnographers actively work to establish rapport and win the trust of their subjects. To this end, they conduct themselves in a nonthreatening and unobtrusive manner. A free and open exchange of thoughts and feelings will be more likely if the ethnographer is perceived as a neutral figure who has no special alliances with groups outside the setting or with individuals in the setting that might harm subjects. No matter how neutrally they are perceived, most fieldworkers are never completely accepted by their subjects (Douglas 1976). Short of conducting covert fieldwork where their research identities are unknown, ethnographers become "marginal natives," part member, part guest. Although not fully accepted, the ethnographer becomes member enough to share the symbols, language, and perspective of the people being studied, to be able to penetrate their defenses against outsiders, and to be seen as a "regular guy" who will "do no one any dirt" (Johnson 1975, 95).

Instead of trying to be a "fly on the wall"—a goal both impossible to achieve and profitless to pursue—we carefully monitor how participants come to regard us. Of course, during the first days in the field, it is common for fieldworkers to "stick out," and for this to affect some or much of the participants' behavior. After two weeks of observation in one laboratory, a technician took Arluke aside privately and told him quite directly that "Jim and the other guys here aren't acting normal, and it's because you're here!" Arluke heard this as bad news, assuming that lab workers were behaving differently around animals. He wondered how many more weeks or months he would have to be present to see how these people actually behaved around lab animals. Sheepishly, and fearing the worst, he asked the technician what was different. She replied, quite happily, that the men in her lab had never treated the female technicians respectfully before, but were doing so now. Stunned and relieved, Arluke shared his fear with the technician that animals were being treated differently because of his presence, to which the technician simply shrugged and said, "Nobody cares about that."

The impact of their presence on participants' behavior and the normal flow of events is limited because field researchers typically are involved with people in their everyday settings. Group members have many things to concern themselves with that are more immediately important than changing their behavior for an ethnographer's benefit. Especially in work settings, people have to do their jobs—clean cages, perform experiments, deal with clients and patients, train animals, and fulfill their other occupational responsibilities—while, at the same time, being aware of the demands and evaluations of their superiors (Becker and Geer 1957).

People's initial curiosity and uneasiness also diminish over time as fieldworkers blend into the settings they study by building rapport with participants. Assuming the role of naive student expedites the process of establishing rapport. Like newcomers in any social situation, fieldworkers must also "learn the roles," a process of initial learning where they "attempt to master where things and people are, the niceties of rank and privilege, who expects him to do what, at what time, for how long; what the rules are—which ones can or must be broken, which followed to the letter" (Geer et al. 1968, 209). Especially in organizational settings, ethnographers are often taken under the wings of workers who act as though they were breaking in new employees. In one primate research lab, for instance, Arluke was warned about "which chimps would throw shit" at him and was given advice about "how to treat the mean ones," to which he nodded thankfully. Soon people let down their guard and increasingly invite fieldworkers to escort them, observe them, or simply hang out with them at work and at other places. The ethnographer moves from being a stranger or a new employee to being a friend as he or she is told gossip and secrets or is asked to join some employees after work for beer.

After learning these basics, fieldworkers immerse themselves in the activities and routines of those studied. This not only allows fieldworkers to experience directly what participants think and feel, but it also may enhance the rapport between them. In his research on animal experimenters, Arluke expected to come and go according to their work schedule, to hang out and socialize with them when permitted, and to help with small tasks such as carrying boxes of equipment or answering the telephone. Even such routine activities provided valuable information. In one setting, he was given the unpopular job of wheeling a cart full of empty mouse cages from the lab to a sterilizing room at the other end of the large medical complex. No one told him how to do this "obvious" task other than

The Human–Animal Tribe

telling him where the sterilizing room was located. As he wheeled the cart down the hallway he became increasingly uncomfortable when people, unconnected to experimentation, passed by. Some stared disapprovingly at the cages, some sniffed in a way that suggested repulsion, and some forthrightly said that they wished there were no animal experimentation in their building. More than once, someone sarcastically quipped, "Here's another mouse killer." Back in the lab, the technicians laughed at his account and said, "Welcome to the club!" He was told to "keep a low profile" and avoid the most direct path to the sterilizing room because it would bring him into contact with administrators, secretaries, and visitors who might give him a hard time. He was advised to take the cart through the empty subterranean basement instead, even though this took five minutes longer. This simple exercise taught Arluke a great deal about how technicians often perceive and deal with critical outsiders (Arluke 1991).

Arluke got more involved with the participants than he expected to, however, when he began his fieldwork; in some of the laboratories he studied, he found himself doing "scut" work that was part of experiments and that often involved close contact with animals. In one mouse lab, his scut work escalated from cleaning animal cages, which entailed handling mice, to carrying out experiments on them. He found himself shaving the hair on mice, punching holes in their ears for identification, measuring the size of their tumors, injecting them with experimental drugs, "sacrificing" them, dissecting them, and disposing of them. This degree of participation proved to be invaluable for both strengthening rapport and learning at firsthand how it felt to work with animals as research "tools."

Self-Reflection

Not all data come from monitoring the activities of others, talking with them about their experiences, and participating in their social world. Researchers acquire the richest data by examining their own experiences, seeing how others react to their in-the-field performances, and attending to the changes in their self concepts as the investigation proceeds. As Susan Krieger (1985, 320) observes:

> I think that often in social research, this is what we really do. We see others as we know ourselves. If the understanding of self is limited and unyielding to change, the understanding of the other is as well. If the understanding of the self is harsh, uncaring and not generous to all the possibilities for being a person, the understanding of the other will show this. The great danger of doing injustice to the reality of the "other" does not come about through use of the self, but through lack of use of a full enough sense of self which, concomitantly, produces a stilted, artificial, limited, and unreal knowledge of others.

A growing body of anthropological and sociological literature critically examines the rhetorical conventions fieldworkers commonly use in their writing. According to this critique, fieldworkers must abandon the idea that they observe the activities of "subjects" "objectively" and use these data to build an authoritative account of a specific social world. Instead, ethnographers are encouraged to recognize the central role they play as participants in the setting and to attend more closely to the emotional and self-shaping aspects of the research experience. Thus, as a source of data, ethnographers also turn inward to their thoughts and feelings that are prompted by their fieldwork.

Certain structural and symbolic features of the human–animal relationship may affect the self-concepts and emotions of those who study it. For example, one of the principal reasons people choose to share their lives with animals is that they perceive an animal's response to a caretaker, unlike the responses of fellow humans, as uniquely simple, honest, loving, and undemanding. Kenneth Shapiro (1989) speaks of the canine-human relationship as premised on the person's viewing the dog as a unique individual with a distinct personality and history.

> History informs the experience of a particular animal whether or not it can tell that history. Events in the life of an animal shape and even constitute him or her. . . . [My dog] is an individual in that he is not

constituted through and I do not live toward him as a species-specific behavioral repertoire or developmental sequence. More positively, he is an individual in that he is both subject to and subject of "true historical particulars.". . . . I cannot replace him, nor, ethically, can I "sacrifice" him for he is a unique individual being.

Features such as these often create strong bonds between owners and their pets and may also emotionally engage fieldworkers who study them. Indeed, it is often noted how quickly humans can feel and show strong emotions for new animals they encounter, and that these feelings are sometimes as intense if not stronger than those felt for humans. We should, then, report and analyze these feelings, should they occur, just as other ethnographers commonly report their emotional involvements with their human informants (e.g., Ellis and Flaherty 1992; Johnson 1975, 155–160; Krieger 1985; Whyte 1955, 288–298).

We believe that these emotions—whether positive or negative— offer fieldworkers a unique opportunity for discovery. Ethnographers can learn an invaluable lesson about the nature of social relationships between animals and people by examining feelings prompted in themselves when in the field. These confrontations with emotion help to bring home, in a very direct way, the close connection between knowing one's self and knowing the social world (cf. Gouldner 1970, 493–495).

In his own research, Sanders often found that feelings of delight, love, and fascination went well beyond the conventional pleasure of discovery he knew in his prior fieldwork. Here, for example, is an excerpt from Sanders' fieldnotes at the end of a day in which he had participated in, and been deeply touched by, the euthanasia of three aged companion animals in the veterinary clinic. The joy of encountering new life overrode the experience of death and loss.

> They anesthetize Pat's shepherd in preparation for the caesarian. I help carry her into the surgery where we place her on her back propped up with a plastic brace. As Martha, Jim, and Linda stand by with towels, Martin makes a large incision and pulls out what looks to be a long, thick, lumpy length of translucent intestine. He

slits it and pulls out a tiny puppy and strips it out of the placenta. He hands it to Linda who puts a rubber bulb in its tiny mouth and sucks out fluid. Then she starts to rub it furiously. Then she holds the puppy's head down and swings it between her legs in a kind of hiking motion (I have been told that the centrifugal force of this move pulls more fluid out of the puppy's lungs). I stand with her as she resumes rubbing—trying to stimulate the puppy to draw its first breath. I am offering the little runty creature—eyes tight shut, wrinkled forehead and muzzle (Martha remarks at one point that the pups look like little manatees)—words of encouragement. Finally, the baby lets out a squeak and begins to move its limbs. We cheer. The same procedure is carried out successfully with two more puppies—two females and one male. The babies are put in a cardboard box in a pile with a heat lamp over it. Jim tells me that they are put in a pile like this because their mutual movements stimulate them. I am very moved. I realize this is a routine event for the rest of the people here, but to me it seems as if these little dead things have been brought back to life. I feel high.

Of course, the human ambivalence toward animals means that researchers may witness actions that leave them feeling uneasy, troubled, or sad. This is especially so when other humans are callous or just indifferent toward animals. At these times, researchers may engage in the same "emotion work" (C. Ellis 1991, 38–43; Hochschild 1983) that the observed do in order to understand their perspective toward animals and how that perspective is influenced by situational norms.

Arluke experienced this in his work on animal researchers. By taking the role of the (human) other, he occasionally found himself acting toward lab animals in ways that mimicked the behavior of those he studied. While this behavior was not blatantly cruel or even neglectful, for the most part, it was often high objectifying, at times involving treatment of the animals as though they did not exist. Caught up in the laboratory's definition of the situation, there were moments when he performed prosaic experiments on rodents. This participation, however, proved unsettling especially when he was away from the lab. Much like Stanley Milgram's (1974) subjects, he found it somewhat distressing to confront how far his "conscience" strayed from the demands of the situation and to acknowledge the moral damage of becoming insensitive, if only for brief periods.

Auto-Ethnography

Ethnographers can also collect information through an approach which, though commonly used years ago by sociologists (e.g., Cooley 1964 [1902], 6–7), has recently regained currency among fieldworkers. While interacting with pets in both public and private settings, researchers can construct "auto-ethnographies," descriptive and introspective accounts detailing their intellectual and emotional experiences (see Denzin 1989; C. Ellis 1991; Hayano 1979). Like conventional ethnographers, auto-ethnographers also work in a multitude of settings and draw upon many resources to focus their research and gain access to the field.

Although studying animals might be new, fieldworkers' studying those with whom they share their lives is not. For example, observing one's own children has frequently provided information on the origin of human social abilities. The classic insights into behavior developed by Charles Darwin (1871) and Charles H. Cooley (1927) were enhanced by observations of their own children. Jean Piaget (1926) and, more recently, Norman Denzin (1977) and Michael McTear (1985) based much of their understanding of the social and psychological development of children on analyses of their offsprings' activities.

Inside auto-ethnography refers to researchers who study situations where they have preexisting personal ties with participants. It contrasts with incursive ethnography, in which researchers enter new situations more or less as strangers. With animals, inside ethnographic work is more likely than incursive work to produce a complete and emotionally informed account, not just of the human perspective, but also that of the animal; it is also less apt to confront researchers with difficult decisions about if, when, and how to intervene. On the other hand, while investigators can usually exit their settings if the experience becomes emotionally painful, the autoethnographer may find this hard to do. Pulling out may not be an option when doing an inside auto-ethnography of a companion animal, since living intimately with one's "subjects" obviously makes it difficult to "leave the field" for rest and reflection. (Other problems and advantages of both types of auto-ethnography have been discussed elsewhere—e.g., Agar 1980; Georges and Jones 1980; Smith and Kornblum, 1989—although not in relation to studying animals.)

Emotional issues may figure prominently in auto-ethnographies of human–animal interactions, particularly when sociologists study their own companion animals. In part, this is due to the intense relationships that can exist between researchers and animals who are defined as "persons," "friends," or "members of the family" (see Beck and Katcher 1983, 39–59; Cain 1985; Veevers 1985; Voith 1983). Sanders experienced this predicament during auto-ethnographic work with his dogs. Still shaken by the death of his last dog, he was often reminded of his old friend and his passing by the new puppies and the materials he was reading. At various points in his fieldnotes, he recorded sorrowful remembrances stirred by the incidents he observed. At other times he found it difficult to continue his study of the puppy kindergarten because of the joyful experiences of being with exuberant puppies. One day he recorded the following in his notes:

> It really strikes me that this is a very different research project from others I have been involved in. I was working on my first paper on it and found myself crying while reading about dog death and its impact on owners. I went out and stood by Cloud's bush and talked to him for a while. I also find myself touched and grinning with pleasure [in the kindergarten] or upset at ineptitude or thoughtless cruelty of the owners. I have never had such an emotional experience with research (except for periods of fear/paranoia when I studied drug use and narcotics enforcers or the transitory stage fright of entering a field situation). There certainly is a difference between being "interested" in a phenomenon or subculture—like my earlier research on tattooing—and feeling positive emotions like love, attachment, and respect.

During their research, fieldworkers only see social structure at a given point in time and space. However, this structure is part of a historical continuity and is intimately related to the world outside the directly observable (Pitt 1972). Use of historical material allows the researcher to understand these prior social worlds. In addition, then, to participant observation, self-reflection, and auto-ethnography, fieldworkers may also try to understand group perspectives even if they existed only in the past. The goal is the same—one tries to represent the participant's point of view whether the participant is alien or domestic, living or dead. The fact that data are fragmentary is also a constant. Just as ethnographers can see only fragments of their cultural field, they can see only the fragments of a time gone by.

Once discovered, these fragments must be contextualized in the broader social world that originally gave them meaning. More than writing general histories that detail and chronicle the events and characters of past worlds, we regard the past as an alien culture and use our sociological imagination to study it. To say that ethnographers represent their subjects' world means that they do not empirically catalog events, but describe and speak about the social processes and systems of meaning that underlie these events and transform particular worlds, in turn making certain statements and deeds possible . We are more interested in meaningful practices than events, ambiguous processes than contained incidents, implicit perspectives than explicit consciousness, ideological concerns than official statement, collective identity than individual story (cf. Comaroff and Comaroff 1992).

To do historical ethnography, the fieldworker must build an archive, working in and outside official records and the established canon of documentary evidence. Although historical subjects cannot directly answer questions or allow for firsthand observation, their lived experience can be examined in archival material such as catalogs, public relations brochures, newsletters, minutes of meetings, correspondence, memos, files, or schedules. These can show, among other things, how an individual or group wanted to be perceived or what the priorities were. Particularly helpful are organizational records, newspapers, oral histories, speeches, laws, and secondary data provided by historians themselves.

Ethnohistory proved invaluable to the writing of this book, although it was a serendipitous undertaking. While doing fieldwork in laboratories, Arluke wanted to compare the experience of experimenting on animals to that of experimenting on humans. As he explored this interest in the literature, he was led to consider the concentration camps of Nazi Germany where physicians performed experiments on inmates. A small point in Robert Lifton's (1986) psychohistory of Nazi physicians was that they sometimes had pets at home that they adored and lavished attention on. To Lifton, this was simply more evidence that these physicians had two separate identities—one at the camps and one at home—that made this inconsistent behavior possible for them. Arluke questioned Lifton's psychologizing and asked whether there might be broader historical and sociological processes in nineteenth- and twentieth-century lying behind this inconsistency.

Understanding Ethnography

Accuracy

The most common criticism leveled by skeptics is that fieldworkers cannot produce "valid" results or accurately represent social phenomena. Although fieldwork has a long and respected history in sociology and anthropology, those unfamiliar with it often accord it little credibility compared to quantitative methods that are seen as more "scientific." What makes the work unscientific, some argue, is that the fieldworker's mere presence alters the normal behavior of participants who act or talk differently with a stranger among them. In addition to such reactivity, others argue that the subjectivity of the fieldworker's biases distorts data collection and their interpretation.

While ethnographers do not conduct experiments in controlled laboratory settings or use prespecified, fixed procedures to collect data, they are concerned about the accuracy of their findings. However, their approach to validity is defined by an interpretive paradigm of research that makes assumptions about "knowing" that are different than those underlying conventional positivist science. In contrast to positivist social scientists whose deductive model proceeds in a linear way from study design to the collection and analysis of data, fieldworkers rely on an inductive, flexible design that is continually redefined and modified. They explore ambiguities and contradictions, allowing data to suggest unanticipated directions. In fact, it is a hallmark of fieldwork to see concepts, hypotheses, and research design emerge as the data are being collected (Lather 1991; Lincoln and Guba 1985).

Also, the fieldworker comprehends and interprets the views and worlds of participants through a reflexive process of appreciation and experiential learning rather than through the collection of "facts" or the controlled observation of "objective" events. While true knowledge does correspond to the phenomena that fieldworkers represent in their writing, they do not expect to obtain the "truth" if that is understood as an independent social reality. Most fieldworkers accept that it is only possible to approximate reality in their writing and allow their readers to judge its likely truth (Hammersley, 1990). The process of describing the realities of other people is complicated by the fieldworker's interest in how actions are conducted, given significance, and work or do not work for participants. Theories and assumptions employed by the fieldworker will guide description, making it impossible for it to be literal and total or for a sharp distinction to be drawn between description and analysis.

Fieldwork, in its final, written form, is a second-order interpretation of what already has been interpreted by the people being studied. This interpretation draws upon participants' constructs as well as those of the fieldworker, or what anthropology calls "emic" and "etic" constructs (Pike, 1954). The emic level of analysis describes what a social world looks and feels like to its members in their own terms. At this level, subjects should be able to see themselves in the data and confirm the ethnographer's take on their world. This kind of confirmation is less likely at the etic level of analysis when ethnographers use categories from outside the culture studied.

The use of both types of constructs can be seen in Arluke and Frederic Hafferty's (1996) research on how dogs are dissected by medical students in physiology class. On the one hand, their work identifies the explanations used by medical students to rationalize their experimentation on dogs, and students would easily acknowledge the accuracy of these descriptions. On the other hand, by drawing on C. Wright Mills' (1940) concept of the "vocabulary of motives,"or the way actors offer explanations for their behavior after they break social conventions, Arluke and Hafferty's research explains sociologically how these justifications can transform students who are initially hesitant about dissecting into enthusiastic dissectors. This analysis involves an etic level of explanation that is useful and understandable to sociologists, but not necessarily to medical students.

Similarly, when dog owners read Sanders' (1990a) description of how people make excuses for their dogs' misbehavior in public, they readily recall personal situations in which they have employed the kinds of justifications discussed. Because they are involved in dealing with immediate situations, however, they typically do not think abstractly about what they are doing. In devising a typology of "excusing tactics" and linking these social maneuvers to a general theory of how disrupted face-to-face interactions affect the actors' social statuses and subsequently require them to offer justifying accounts, Sanders moves to an etic level of discussion.

Fieldworkers hope to provide emic descriptions that most participants can confirm. Techniques such as the "members' test" are used in which researchers show their writing to subjects for critique and modification (Bloor 1983). The careful fieldworker will, of course, also cross-check the reports of one informant against another's and will pay close attention to discrepancies. Perhaps the best assurance of validity is for the fieldworker to "triangulate," collecting different types of data on the same issue. Arluke, for instance, collected three kinds of data in his study of animal experimenters. First, he directly

The Human–Animal Tribe

examined the behavior of people in thirty-five labs. Each visit lasted from one week to a year and involved unrestricted observation of all human–animal contacts of an experimental, caretaking, or socializing nature, as well as observation of formal (e.g., veterinary rounds, staff meetings) and informal (e.g., office talk, parties, breaks) human interaction. He made additional observations, for shorter periods, in many other facilities. Second, as noted above, he participated in the life and work of laboratories, at times assisting in experimentation and animal handling, and always trying to fit in with the local culture as much as possible. And third, he deliberately and formally conducted open-ended, semistructured interviews with 185 subjects long after rapport had emerged, thus ensuring the most revealing and honest responses. He held these interviews with almost every person he encountered in the field, from secretaries to principal investigators. Moreover, in each interview, he made it explicitly clear than anonymity would be provided in exchange for cooperation and candor. (In such circumstances, it is standard practice not to identify specific sources of quotations or name specific settings studied; to do otherwise would be unethical.) Consequently, virtually all interviews achieved a high level of cooperation, with many lasting more than three hours. To date, he has compiled approximately fifteen hundred pages of detailed field observations and has transcribed approximately four thousand pages of interviews.

As time progresses, the participants' view of fieldworkers changes considerably—a process all newcomers undergo as they become more like members than visitors. Significantly, playing these roles does not lessen the accuracy of the studies but enhances them by showing how researchers become embedded in the field and what kinds of data then become available. Arluke assumed a variety of roles in his research on the culture of animal experimentation, including friend, coworker, confidante, gofer, and witness. In the latter role, he found himself invited by some labs to observe researchers conducting experiments on animals. In these instances, he was, even in the beginning, a most welcome guest. His subjects, believing that their work with animals fully conformed to governmental and institutional regulations, wanted him to witness their behavior so the public would learn this from an "objective" outsider (cf. Bosk 1985).

In studying the veterinary clinic, Sanders increasingly came to participate in the kinds of tasks usually relegated to veterinary assistants. He helped restrain patients, 'held veins' as blood was drawn, carried anesthetized animals into surgery, positioned animals for X-rays, and in a variety of other ways assisted in the necessary work of the hospital. At one level, this assumption of the quasi-assistant role made sense because it provided direct experience of, and access to, a variety of interactions with animal patients. Sanders' helping out was also appreciated by the clinic staff and they, therefore, were more willing to speak honestly and openly with him about the often-sensitive issues he was exploring. But Sanders' direct participation in the work of the clinic was prompted by far more than the mere desire to acquire rich and varied field data. He felt an obligation: the clinic's doctors and staff allowed him essentially unrestricted access to their setting and work lives. In return, and because over time the staff members became his friends, and he sympathized with them in their rushed and underpaid labors, he felt it only fair to help them out.

Indeed, in certain respects, the fieldworker's data and interpretation may be more credible than those of the quantitative researcher. Fieldwork data are less artifactual or reactive than either experimental or survey data because fieldworkers study people in their natural situations subject to the everyday constraints operating there (Emerson, 1983). Experiments and surveys, however, create artificial situations with researcher-defined parameters imposed on the people studied.

Fieldworkers, in fact, may far outstrip quantitative researchers when it comes to studying emotionally charged or highly sensitive issues, as those in human–animal interaction often are. Quantitative methods using fixed and highly structured questions to survey large numbers of respondents may at best just skim the surface of meaning and at worst highly distort it. This is because quantitative researchers may have little if any rapport with participants. Indeed, these researchers sometimes never meet their subjects in person or directly experience their lives. Simply asking people what they think and feel does not always yield answers that correspond to their actual behavior and reactions, since they may reply with what they think is the right or safe response or attempt to project a socially desirable image of themselves (Deutscher 1973). The ethnographer, on the other hand, can directly observe participants' behavior and establish relationships with them that encourage openness during interviews. Even if willing to talk openly, people are not always able to articulate thoughts and feelings that are unexamined or taken for granted. The quantitative researcher, removed from the field, cannot begin to understand these deeply embedded meanings. These hidden pieces of information, however, can be addressed by the ethnograher who has been in the field long enough to learn and experience these hard-to-articulate elements of culture.

A case in point is Arluke's field research in animal shelters where many aspects of human–animal relations could not have been tapped had he merely distributed a questionnaire. Only by participating in the shelter's social world did he learn what staff members took for granted regarding their work. After six months in the field, for instance, Arluke began to understand what shelter workers really thought and felt about euthanizing animals. For some time he observed that, when they discussed the propriety of euthanasia, a mild degree of tension developed between those who routinely euthanized animals and those who did not. Those who did the euthanizing seemed to resent others who commented, judged, or ridiculed it. But the meaning of this tension was unclear even when workers were asked about it directly. Months of fieldwork made it possible for Arluke to see that there was an unarticulated belief behind this tension; namely, that no one really understands what it is like to euthanize shelter animals, why it is necessary, and how it can be done "well," unless they have actually done it themselves. Therefore, no one else has the "right" to say much about it. Without the special knowledge imparted by experience, those who have never euthanized were believed to be ill equipped to rule on most aspects of euthanasia. But they did so, nevertheless; hence the tension.

Generalizability and Insight

Some have sought to discredit ethnography on the grounds that it produces ungeneralizable results because the sampling of settings and subjects lacks system and breadth. Although its labor-intensive method limits the number of study settings, labeling fieldwork as "merely anecdotal" or, more flatteringly, as an "insightful case study," ignores the rigor of its methods. Ethnographers would argue that field studies, even if not generalizable, report data that may be far more accurate than those that result from surveys of many people and settings. But the generalizability of field studies should not be sold short. Ethnographers can see each setting and subject as both unique and similar because they study the manifestation of general social processes in specific circumstances. As windows on society, all individuals and settings are representative of all others (Bogdan and Taylor 1975). When some people or settings more clearly demonstrate certain processes than others, the researcher must find the ones that best illustrate the project's sociological focus.

Ideally, fieldwork should not end until the researcher reaches "saturation"—a state where everything one sees and hears has been encountered before (Shaffir et al. 1980, 257–310). Reaching that point means that the additional data being collected merely add bulk rather than enrich the analysis, and that one is no longer finding negative cases that question or alter the patterns discovered (Becker and Geer 1960; Glaser and Strauss 1967). To reach this point, fieldworkers typically remain in the field long enough to have seen all possible variations in behavior. When studying a reasonably small group of people, everyone can be observed, but with larger groups, the fieldworker may have to sample different time periods and subgroups to ensure that everything bearing on the researcher's focus has been encountered and understood.

For some, the real problem with fieldwork may be that it gets things "too right." Some who challenge it may be responding, at least in part, to the discomfort precipitated by having to face who they really are as a group or by having this description passed on to the public. Fieldwork is an attempt to understand a group's way of life; it is a form of analysis that yields insight at a cultural level. Yet few people, as individuals or as members of a group, are comfortable being analyzed. The analysis may be felt as an unwelcome intrusion into something not public; it may be seen as dangerous because it can provide fodder for those critical of one's way of life; and it may be upsetting to face things that one may have chosen or learned not to face. In a sense, then, field research is always "subversive" in that it questions the group's conventional image and looks behind its acceptable—or most reputable—presentation of itself (Becker 1967).

Arluke ran into exactly this problem with his research on animal experimenters. Although he found striking evidence of guilt in some, but not all, of those he studied, he met substantial resistance and denial when he attempted to report this finding to them. The problem he had with titles for his talks and articles is a good example of this. Several years ago he was invited to speak at a conference of animal researchers, and chose to call his talk, "The Experimenter's Guilt." He was told that this choice was "too controversial" and he should change it to "Stress Among Researchers." When this paper was submitted for possible publication in a laboratory animal journal, one of the reviewers said that the term "stress" was hyperbolic and that the article would give "ammunition to the enemy." So he changed the title to "Uneasiness Among Laboratory Technicians," and it was published after many quotations were deleted or changed by the editors (Arluke 1990b). Two years after publication, he was asked to speak about the same topic at a major pharmaceutical company, but learned that he could not use "uneasiness" in the title because it would "inflame the research directors." A more nondescript title, "How Researchers Deal with their Feelings," was preferred.

We see field research as predominantly (at best) a way to wonder about culture. Cultural knowledge, like self-knowledge, permits the knower to put thoughts and feelings into some context, to inspect them, and to gain power over them. Perhaps this sort of wondering offers the most relevant criterion for evaluating field research—does the research provide new and useful interpretations and insights?

Such knowledge is useful, we would argue, if it surprises us or makes us stop and wonder before we proceed with our regular thoughts and actions. Certainly, not facing what people actually think and feel is potentially the most dangerous approach if we hope to inform and shape our future. Thus, the end result of fieldwork is that it can enlarge our understandings of ways of life previously misunderstood or simply unexplored.

Take animal experimentation, for example. People are very concerned that laboratory animals be treated humanely by scientists. Yet currently, the general public knows very little about what really goes on between experimenters and their animals. As with most emotionally charged issues, people on both sides of this debate tend to caricature their opponents, making them into enemies whose stereotyped beliefs and actions fit their expectations. Such distortion is not only incorrect, it is dangerous because it adds fuel to a fire that, if continuously stoked, makes communication more difficult than it already is. To demystify this element of the animal experimentation controversy, it is necessary to open up the world of the biomedical researcher so the public can see the process of animal experimentation and step inside the shoes of the people who do this work. Any real attempt to improve the handling and treatment of laboratory animals certainly would require detailed information about the people who work with them. Answers to basic questions about the people who design and conduct animal experiments, as well as those who care for experimental animals, would seem to be a first step in the development of new and informed policies and alternatives regarding laboratory animal care. Yet at the moment, we know very little about what actually goes on in research laboratories—a situation that calls for the ethnographer's trained eyes.

Clearly, ethnography has enormous potential for generating insight into how humans regard animals. But its insight-generating potential can be even greater if sociologists are willing to rethink some of their discipline's tired assumptions. We challenge some of these assumptions in the next chapter.

The Human–Animal Tribe

chapter 2

Learning from Animals

> If lions could speak, we could not understand them.
>
> —Ludwig Wittgenstein, *Philosophical Investigations*

STUDYING OUR CULTURE'S ATTITUDES toward animals follows the long-standing ethnographic tradition of documenting the perspective of humans. In this chapter, we explore a less traditional issue: Is it possible to capture the animal's perspective and, if so, how does one go about it? In weighing this possibility, we need to reexamine certain assumptions underlying conventional sociological thinking about, and fieldwork with, humans. Representing the animal's perspective requires that investigators become intimately involved with the animal-other and carefully attuned to their emotional experience. This unique research promises to expand our sociological understanding of how "mind" results from social interaction, how identities are assigned to others, and how to go about taking the role of the other when one actor ostensibly cannot use conventional symbols. We argue that seeing the world through an animal's eyes can

lead ethnographers to abandon their traditional objective, nonjudgmental stance. Knowledge of the animal's situation may prompt direct—and, we maintain, appropriate—intervention.

Animals as Minded Social Actors

Sociologists typically have seen mind and the social self as dependent
upon the special human ability to assume the viewpoint of those with
whom one interacts. From a conventional sociological standpoint,
the presumed inability to symbolize means that the nonhuman animal lacks all the supposedly unique human attributes associated
with linguistic facility. From this anthropocentric perspective, the
animal can think only in the most rudimentary ways, does not possess a self-concept, has no sense of time or space, cannot plan future
actions apart from the boundaries imposed by the immediate situation, cannot differentiate between ends and means, and has no "emotions" in the sense that the animal cannot indicate these feelings to
the self or to others. Trapped in the here and now, the nonhuman
animal habitually or instinctively responds to stimuli presented in
the immediate situation (see E. Becker 1981, 94; Mead 1964 [1934],
154–169; cf. Terrace 1987).

This alleged "understanding" of the "life–world" of nonhuman
animals is, we would argue, derived more from anthropocentric ideology than from systematically derived data or thoughtful examination of analysts' personal experiences (if such exist) with nonhuman
animals. The effect of such human-centered (anthropocentric) ideology is just as distorting as male-centered (androcentric) ideology
has been to gaining an understanding of women and their experience. Feminist critics of anthropology maintain that ethnographers
have ignored women or have perceived them as silent and passive.
As Susan Gal (1991, 189) notes, "Being unable to express their struc-
turally generated views in the dominant and masculine discourse,
women were neither understood nor heeded, and became inarticu-
late, 'muted' or even silent." Only recently have researchers sought

The Human–Animal Tribe

to understand the meaning of this silence and to study "women's voice" (e.g., di Leonardo 1991).

Once one acquires sympathetic understanding through the process of interacting directly with those who are studied, the "alien" behavior comes to be seen as commonplace and eminently reasonable. Some investigators of the animal–human relationship have advocated the use of interpretive, phenomenologically sensitive, qualitative approaches to acquire such an understanding of animals. For example, Harold Herzog and Gordon Burghardt (1988, 91–92) observe:

> The concept of consciousness as a topic of scientific scrutiny, even in animals, is making a comeback. . . . There are some important questions that can only be investigated by studying subjective reports of conscious experience. . . . We concur and suggest that methods that phenomenologists use to investigate "being in the world" might be fruitfully applied to the study of human–animal relationships.

Trainers, many ethologists, and others who interact consistently and intimately with animals outside the artificial situations of conventional scientific inquiry, typically see their nonhuman associates as self-aware, planning, empathetic, emotional, complexly communicative, and creative (e.g., George 1985; Goodall 1986; Hearne 1987; Shapiro 1990a; Strum 1987). True familiarity with the complexities of animal behavior prompts them to discount perspectives that rely on instinctual or rigidly behavioristic explanations. As Mary Midgley (1988, 39) observes in her discussion of cognitive ethologist Donald Griffin's work: "The attempt to make pre-programming account for everything has only been made to look plausible by constant misdescription—by abstract, highly simplified accounts of what creatures do, which are repeatedly shown up as inadequate when anybody takes the trouble to observe them longer and more carefully."

The dog owners Sanders studied regularly described interactions with their dogs that to them clearly and reasonably demonstrated the animals' ability to be thoughtful, insightful, and empathic. They characterized their dogs typically as creatively employing learned gestural signs in symbolic ways; they organized their behavior to communicate new ideas in novel situations. For example, one client in a veterinary clinic spoke of her dog's ability to "talk."

> He talks to me all the time. He has different barks for different things—to tell me things. When someone is at the door, he has this deep, big-dog bark. When he is frightened, he has this real high bark. Yes, he can talk. When he really wants something, he turns circles. You ask him if he wants to go for a ride in the car, he will turn circles and run to the garage door. If you ask him a question and his answer is "yes," he will turn circles. If his answer is "no," he just sits there and looks at you and you have to keep asking questions until you hit on it.

In a similar vein, animal trainer Vicki Hearne (1987, 55–56) describes an incident in which her dog Salty creatively directs the conversation of gestures to establish a new definition of intention.

> At this point in Salty's training it is not clear whether the utterance "Salty, Sit!" is language, even though there is plainly a looped thought involved: Salty, that is, is sitting in response to her recognition of my intention that she do so. . . . We have a looped thought, but the flow of intention is, as it were, one way. In my account the dog doesn't initiate anything yet. She obeys me, but I don't obey her. One day, though, and quite soon, I am wandering around the house and Salty gets my attention by sitting spontaneously in just the unmistakably symmetrical, clean-edged way of formal work. If I'm on the ball, if I respect her personhood at this point, I'll respond. Her sitting may have a number of meanings. "Please stop daydreaming and feed me!" (Perhaps she sits next to the Eukanuba or her food dish.) Or it may mean, "Look, I can explain about the garbage can, it isn't the way it looks." In any case, if I respond, the flow of intention is now two-way, and the meaning of "Sit" has changed yet again. This time it is Salty who has enlarged the context . . . Salty and I are, for the moment at least, obedient to each other and to language.

In contrast to conventional positivistic assumptions about the interactional capabilities and emotional experience of nonhuman animals (see Hebb 1946), there is considerable evidence that dogs and other animals with whom humans routinely interact do possess at least a rudimentary ability to "take the role of the other"; and they behave in ways that are purposefully intended to shape interactions to accomplish their defined goals or communicate an understanding of their associates' subjective experience. Sanders' informants, for example, commonly described their dogs as being aware of and responsive to their moods. Typical accounts detailed incidents in which the caretaker was sad or depressed and the dog, recognizing this emotional state, behaved in ways intended to console or display concern. At heart, the social exchange between the person and the companion animal was defined as an "emotive discourse" (Gubrium 1986). Sanders interviewed a man and his teenaged daughter, who spoke of their dog's empathetic capacities.

> *Daughter*: He's just fun. He keeps us lighthearted. And he certainly senses our moods. If you're sad and crying, he will come snuggle next to you.
>
> *Father*: He just seems to sense it somehow. You can be in a different room and be down. Recently when Mary was in her room, he just seemed to know where to go. . . . He sensed that somewhere in this house—his doghouse—there was something that was not quite right. He sought Mary out and was just there. One day I was sitting on the front porch kind of blue about some things, and he just snuggled in there—totally uninvasive. Just, "If you want to pet me, pet me. I'm here if you need me."

Further support for the social abilities of dogs and other animal companions comes from their commonly taking objects from their immediate environment, purposefully redefining the material item in a new way, and acting toward the object in light of this redefinition. For example, in the auto-ethnographic notes recorded following a walk in the woods with his own dogs, Sanders described the animals at play and the implications of what he had observed.

> In addition to "chase" and "wrestle" (in which they assume and reverse roles—chaser and chasee, aggressor and victim—according to a mutual understanding which I haven't as yet figured out), the dogs have established a game I have started to call "stick." One of them—usually Emma—chooses a stick which has no obvious

intrinsic value relative to all the others in the woods other than it is the "right" size—usually about a foot long and easily held in the mouth. This stick becomes the major game piece. The chooser displays the stick with great gestural show of its importance—head up, tail high, body tensed, gaze directed at the other "player." In turn, the other, usually after some display of mock indifference, chases after the "holder" and attempts to take it away. When successful, the roles are reversed and the new holder attempts to keep the stick from the new chaser. They have even established a conventional stick-holding style, which both use and which has an obvious utility given the rudimentary rules of the game. The stick is usually held lengthwise so that most of it extends out of one side of the holder's mouth. By turning her head or body, the holder can stay in close contact with the other player but can position the graspable part of the stick away from the enthusiastic chaser. This would seem to be an interesting example of the symbolic redefinition of a natural object, mutual definition of the situation, ability to take the role of the other, and the sharing of an activity characterized by mutually agreed-upon rudimentary rules.

Recent field studies by primatologists support the reasonableness of seeing nonhuman animals as having minds, behaving intentionally, and being attuned to their own and their fellows' emotional experience. Dorothy Cheney and Robert Seyfarth (1990), for instance, maintain that much can be learned about what it is like to be a vervet monkey. Vervet calls, they argue, are far more than mere involuntary expressions of emotion; instead, they are given only when there is an appropriate audience to hear them (i.e., fellow vervets). Vervets also deal with relations such as transitivity and generalize kin relations so that females, when played a juvenile's [recorded] distress call, will look at the mother of that juvenile. Cheney and Seyfarth (1991) also contend that these monkeys' deception of other monkeys probably means that they can conceive of others' differing viewpoints. Nevertheless, the authors warn that monkeys probably do not attribute mental states to other monkeys. Studies of chimpanzees, in contrast, seem to suggest that they have more of a true "theory of mind" (Menzell and Halperin 1975; Premack and

Woodruff 1978); these primates aid, share, inform, and deliberately misinform. Further, George Gallup's (1982) experimental research persuasively shows that the chimpanzee possesses a rudimentary self-concept.

Studies of apes who have learned American Sign Language may provide further support for this argument, although there is no consensus in the scientific community as to what these language capabilities mean. Those who champion ape language abilities maintain that these animals can construct a world with words, retrieve and communicate past experiences, and even discuss the nature of life (Laidler 1980; Meddin 1979; Patterson and Linden 1981). Critics of ape language research (e.g., Chomsky 1980; Sebeok 1981), perhaps desiring to retain one ability that differentiates humans from nonhuman animals, disagree with the implications of these studies.

If nonhuman animals are thoughtful, or minded, social actors, then what method can fieldworkers use to study them? In certain circumstances, it is essential for the investigator to learn how to take the role of the animal-other and communicate effectively in the appropriate idiom. According to ethologist Margaret Nice (quoted in Lawrence, 1989:118), "A necessary condition for success . . . is a continuous sympathetic observation of an animal under as natural conditions as possible. To some degree, one must transfer oneself into the animal's situation and inwardly partake in its behavior." For example, in his study of feral cats, Roger Tabor (1983) credits his acceptance as a "participant observer" to his ability to speak what he terms "pidgin-cat." He learned to use the gestures and make the sounds he saw were significant to the members of the animal community in which he was interested. Kenneth Shapiro (1990b), who calls his approach "kinesthetic empathy," suggests a "mixed" methodology, using knowledge of the individual animal's history and its social construction to understand the animal's postures, movements, and use of space. Such empathy is not mere anthropomorphizing or projecting, he contends, since humans share with animals an awareness and intelligence based on respective bodily movement, giving humans and nonhuman animals an "embodied consciousness" regarding our shared ways of knowing the world through movement. Similarly, Henry Blake (1975) and Hearne (1987), in their training work with horses and dogs, and Dian Fossey (1983), Jane Goodall (1986), and Shirley Strum (1987), in their ethological studies of free-ranging primates, stress the central methodological and practical importance of learning to speak and behave appropriately, given the values and expectations of the animals with whom one is interacting.

As Sanders' research into the animal–human relationship proceeded, for example, he learned to move, verbalize, and respond in ways which were appropriately communicative and understandable to the canine actors in the research settings. He derived elements of this understanding from reading ethological accounts (e.g., Brandenburg 1988; Lorenz [1953] 1988) and the practical literature directed at dog owners interested in communicating effectively with their animals (e.g., Baer 1989; George 1985; Ross and McKinney 1992). But the information most useful for "learning to talk" came from his direct observations of the dogs as they interacted. He routinely engaged in what Nancy Mandell (1988) refers to as "action reproduction" as the grounding of communication. He became adept at elemental canine communication by disclosing his own desires, perspectives, and plans of action through whines, growls, nuzzling, ear-sniffing, body postures, nipping, facial expression, and the other communicative moves that he saw the dogs use frequently and effectively with one another. Sanders commonly assumed what might be called the "least-human role" (see Mandell's 1988 discussion of her nursery-school research), attempting to minimize species differences and assume the perspective of the animals.

Answering the Skeptic

While the view of nonhuman animals as minded is controversial in the animal behavior literature (see Clark 1984; Griffin 1984; Ristau 1991), it is closer to heresy among sociological determinists and tra-

The Human–Animal Tribe

ditional symbolic interactionists (see Cohen 1989; Lindesmith et al. 1977, 63–80, 115–126). In his critical discussion of the current state of sociological social psychology, James Dowd (1991, 201) contends that seeing nonhuman animals as capable of using shared symbols and engaging in minded behavior is as threatening to the underpinnings of traditional symbolic interactionism as is the questioning of the autonomous human self in contemporary postmodern analysis.

Indeed, many people would insist that the study of the animal's perspective could only be anthropomorphic (e.g., Hilbert 1994): no matter what, the existence of animal minds is sheer projection. Many use the term "projection" to mean a kind of falsification, mistaking what is inside the observer for what one sees in the subject. As mere human projections, it is argued, all we can learn in studying animals is more about the human mind. Indeed, some would say that even the "fact" of human mindedness is as questionable a piece of ideology as is our position that nonhuman animals engage in minded behavior.

Understanding animals does not require us to conceive of "mind" as an "object" (i.e., a linguistically constituted internal conversation) "possessed" by nonhuman animals or people. We strongly believe that mind is a social accomplishment (Sanders 1993; see also Gubrium 1986). The most appropriate route to understanding social interaction, therefore, be it human-to-human or nonhuman-to-human, is to focus on collective action as practical and premised on interactants' (often mistaken, typically tentative) estimates of how others understand what is going on and how they would like things to proceed. Because the study of communication between humans and nonhuman animals means attributing some linguistic ability to animals, critics may be concerned that we label too much as animal language, and that doing so is the "grossest anthropocentrism of all." We acknowledge the obvious linguistic differences between humans and animals, while asking how animal mindedness might be approached from a nonpositivist perspective that sees animals as more than behavioristic machines (see Wieder 1980). Although animals cannot speak to us in our own terms, we must not throw up our hands and conclude that crossing species barriers and understanding animals' experience is impossible. There are humans whose verbal abilities are severely limited or absent, yet ethnographers have sought to penetrate these minds too, as in the Melvin Pollner and Lynn McDonald-Wikler's (1985) study of how a family attributed normality to a severely retarded child, by interpreting the intention behind her behavior and "speaking for" her in certain situations. Because animals are seen as language deficient in human terms, the social scientific community suffers from a bias that minimizes animal "intelligence" and draws overly rigid boundaries between humans and other animals. To accept this bias leaves one forever locked in the same human categories of communicating and knowing, denying the possible discovery of animal-based or animal-sensitized categories.

On the other hand, the skeptics might be right; the view that animal companions can engage in minded, self-presenting, and intersubjective social interaction may be presumption or it may be projection. But the evidence employed by those who routinely define the intentions of animals and make judgments about their internal states is as persuasive as that employed to establish the intersubjectivity of human-to-human interaction (cf. Bogdan and Taylor 1989; Gubrium 1986; Schutz 1970, 163–217). It would seem reasonable, then, to acknowledge that human–animal interaction can have a mutuality based on the animal's self-awareness and ability to, at least at some rudimentary level, empathically experience the perspective of coactors. The explanatory value of these factors is at least as powerful as causal accounts solely premised on behaviorist or instinctivist presumptions. D. Lawrence Wieder (1980, 95), for example, describes this mutual orientation at the heart of routine animal–human interaction in his discussion of the relationship between researchers who work directly with chimpanzees (or "chimpers") and their primate colleagues:

> The chimpanzee's body in a spatially surrounding world is experienced as intersubjective—as there for both chimp and chimper. . . . Within this common intersubjective Nature, the chimper's body obtains its sense as a body "over there" for the chimp. He or she perceives that body and, through it, perceives the chimper. Implicit here

is a mutual "being for one another." The chimper experiences himself or herself as experienced. Fixed through mutual gazes and such behaviors as hiding one's face and turning away, the chimpanzee is experienced as actively witnessing the chimper and his or her comportment—indeed, this underlies much chimping strategy. The chimper also experiences fellow chimpers and other chimpanzees as Others for the chimp in question and notes that this chimp is an Other for them as well.

We would like skeptics to ask a more "constructive" question: Given the possibilities and constraints of studying the animal mind, what standards of scholarship might be acceptable to our community? For example, what constitute acceptable data in discussions of animal mind? While any attempt to construct theory does violence to what is theorized, this chapter advocates the massing of diverse data from settings in which people and animals interact in order to build a general, sociologically informed description of human–animal exchange. Nor should we undervalue much of these data, even though they do not constitute conventional "scholarship." What makes us take an observation seriously is not the eloquence of its writing, but rather the nature of the author's relationships with animals. Just as we attribute truth and accuracy to ethnographic research based on the quality of the investigator's relationships with those studied and the credibility of his or her account (Hammersley, 1990, 54–72), it is reasonable to use the same criteria in evaluating studies of animal-human interaction. The extent and quality of the relationship a person—whether a social scientist or not—has with the animals being studied, as well as how rigorously and systematically he or she amasses information, should be the central issues in judging the "truth value" of such studies.

Finally, some might argue (e.g., Hilbert 1994) that our attention should be redirected at "sentience" instead of "mind," and the more appropriate presumption would be that humans are animals rather than that nonhuman animals behave like humans in certain circumstances. We agree that there is a shared "animality" of humans and nonhuman creatures and also that much can be learned by exploring these commonalities. However, glossing over significant differences between humans and nonhuman animals—as done by some sociobiologists—may lead to ideologically and empirically questionable conclusions (e.g., human aggression and sexual inequalities are "natural" and therefore justified); on the other hand, anthropomorphically portraying them as far more similar to humans than they actually are does nonhuman animals a disservice. Elizabeth Marshall Thomas (1993) demonstrates this latter failing in her "research-based" speculations about the subjective experience of domestic dogs. Focusing, then, on the "sentience" common to humans and nonhuman animals is, we maintain, overly expansive. While focusing on "feelings and sensations" is interesting and can lead to sociologically significant insights, our intention in this chapter has been to set and focus the aim of those researchers who want to challenge Ludwig Wittgenstein's (1958, 223) contention that we could not understand lions if they were to speak.

Understanding and Intervention

As more is learned about the orientations, behaviors, feelings, and requirements of animals and the perspectives of humans that live and work with them, researchers are more likely to encounter situations that make them want to intervene. They may see or hear things that offend their personal sensibilities or, worse, violate larger moral codes or formal laws. When fieldworkers become important witnesses to beliefs and behaviors that might otherwise go unreported or even undetected by outsiders, the traditional rule in sociology is not to intervene. After all, the fieldworkers' primary goal is to capture a group's perspective and treat it as "neither true nor false, good nor bad" (Bogdan and Taylor 1975, 9). Beliefs, biases, and judgments that might distort this learning process must be suspended.

When fieldworkers adhere to the "silent witness" convention, because of their promises of anonymity or other reasons, they must learn to deal in other ways with their "guilty knowledge." In order to justify their hands-off stance, researchers often argue that more worthwhile changes may be obtained through publication of their work and its dissemination to interested parties who are in a better position to make necessary changes. Thus, when it comes time to write up and publish one's results, the trust of those studied is not betrayed because individuals and settings are rarely named or specifically identified in reports. Instead, fieldworkers generalize about social types and processes, hoping that by reaching a wide audience insights will be considered and perhaps implemented in settings like those directly studied. So, in exchange for not blowing the whistle on a few individuals, fieldworkers trust that greater change will result elsewhere. They also justify their stance by maintaining that intervention might jeopardize their continued access, and this, of course, might well be so. If ethnographers violated the research bargains they negotiated by reporting immoral, unethical, or illegal behavior, participants would reasonably become suspicious of their intent, thus making continued access unlikely and entry into new settings far more difficult.

However, even when field researchers focus on relatively powerless groups or subordinate members of organizations, they are still not examining groups that, like animals, have literally no access to power or ability to express concerns. When researchers work in situations of such extreme inequality, moral and ethical questions raised in the field may trouble ethnographers deeply. Is it moral to remain unobtrusive and mute while animals are being treated in ways that are contrary to personal standards, established institutional norms, or the law? The sensitive ethnographer investigating human-animal relationships may well conclude that it is appropriate to exercise "conscious partiality" (Mies 1983), instead of maintaining a neutral stance.

Much of the impetus for intervention in the power relationships integral to the field situations in which ethnographers work comes from feminist critiques of conventional science and the objectivist methodological stance central to scientific dogma. Feminist scholars emphasize how gender has shaped what is "known" about the social world and increasingly have come to advocate a new way of seeing that is grounded in naturalistic methods and rejects the masculinist preconceptions underlying traditional social theories (see Cook and Fonow 1986; Gorelick 1991; Haraway 1989; Keller 1985; Tanner 1981; Zihlman 1978). Feminist writers also have refocused perspectives on both the means and the ends of the research endeavor. Naturalistic, participatory, emotionally focused, self-attentive approaches lead necessarily to the collection of information that is emancipatory and reconstructs views on the place of humans in nature. Intervention in destructive patterns of domination—domination of the natural environment (Diamond and Orenstein 1990; Plant 1989) and domination on the basis of racial, ethnic, economic, gender, and species categories—is an ethical mandate integral to the research process. In this light, emancipatory involvement directed at easing the lot of animals in the myriad settings in which they interact with, and are dominated by, humans is an essential—though problematic—goal (see Adams 1990; Donovan 1990).

While the human relationship with animals often assumes idealized proportions (Perin 1981), it is, as we have said, an ambivalent one that is also characterized by neglect and cruelty. Animals can be seen as entertaining objects, "filthy" pests, or a good meal while also being regarded as almost human. As objects, they may be treated with rancor and disregard and, as valued coactors, they may be treated with kindness and compassion. Inequality is integral to human relationships with animals, and when ethnographers encounter this inequality, they may be inclined to intervene.

For example, as Sanders' research proceeded and his understanding of canine behavior increased, he was frequently struck by the ignorance, thoughtless disregard, and unwise kindness of dog owners. Dogs were punished for being confused, they were overfed, allowed to engage in dangerous behavior, given conflicting signals, and not rewarded for their honest attempts to understand and respond appropriately to owners' demands. Initially, he simply watched and recorded. As his discomfort grew, however, he decided that he had an ethical responsibility for the welfare of the "subordinates" in the human–animal dyad (see Galliher 1980) and came to exercise "conscious partiality." In giving advice about feeding, explaining dogs' behavior to their caretakers, offering an interpretation of the animals' perspective, and advocating more effective training techniques, he eased his own discomfort and fulfilled what he came to see as his moral responsibility.

Arluke had similar experiences during his research on animal experimenters, although his mode of intervention was somewhat different. He found that simply asking questions that allowed people to reflect on their work in a nonjudgmental atmosphere sometimes prompted critical self-reflection. Through interviewing, he was able to reinforce and encourage respondents to take the animals' perspective, especially in those instances where people had felt uncomfortable taking such a view. When they seemed insensitive or numbed to the plight of a laboratory animal, at the appropriate moments, respondents were gently challenged to rethink their actions toward animals. Finally, in the rare cases when neglect or abuse was discovered, Arluke questioned individuals about their behavior and, if they were unresponsive, at the end of his study he informed those who would be more receptive to and take responsibility for the misbehavior toward the animals. What was particularly important, however, was to relay his information to the right insiders—key staff members, ranking high enough in the hierarchy to voice these concerns legitimately and yet not endanger their own jobs by intervening.

The study of animal-human interaction promises many rewards. The first would be the expansion of sociological thinking and research to include relationships with nonhuman, though minded, social beings. A central proposition here is that the difference between the abilities of people and nonhuman animals—a perceived difference that has thus far excluded animals from serious sociological attention—is a matter of degree rather than kind. It is only through acknowledging that our animal companions are eminently conscious partners in social interaction that we will come to examine and understand their perspectives and behaviors. This understanding can be achieved only if we make the same assumption that qualitative researchers make when they investigate other alien, though knowable, minds and worlds. Intimate interaction and empathy with the perspective of the other are the major sources of this knowledge.

The endeavor advocated here can, we believe, significantly expand our understanding of how mind is constituted. Empathetic, disciplined investigation of the routine social exchanges between people and their nonhuman companions necessarily focuses on how human actors construct (or avoid constructing) an understanding of the animal-other's subjective experience. Thus, the concept of mind is moved beyond the conventional social psychological orientation in which mind is an "object" constituted in the internal conversation of the individual actor. In contrast, examination of human–animal interactions leads to a far more social perspective on mind; it is reconceived as the product of interaction in which intimates are actively involved in contextualizing, identifying, understanding, and responding to the defined subjective experience of the nonverbal other. Human–animal research can, therefore, build upon and expand the somewhat more conventional investigations of interactions with other nonverbal human actors such as infants (e.g., Brazelton 1984), Alzheimer's patients (e.g., Gubrium 1986), and those with severe physical and mental disabilities (e.g., Bogdan and Taylor 1989; Goode 1992).

This refocused attention to mindedness as a feature of sociogenic identity opens the way to an expanded understanding of a variety of other key symbolic interactionist concepts and concerns. For example, how does one understand another's perspective when he or she cannot, or will not, talk about it? How do people define situations in order to make sense of the interactions in which they are involved? What is the role of emotional experience in the structuring of intersubjective encounters?

Examining the animal's perspective can do more than merely enlarge the corpus of sociological theory and method. A far broader and ultimately more important goal is to counter the masculinist, positivist, structuralist, reductionist view of the natural world and the place of "man" within it. Interpretive–experiential involvement in the exchanges between people and animals provides an opportunity to reconstruct the world of nature. As Donna Haraway (1992, 297) writes: "The actors are not all 'us.' If the world exists for us as 'nature,' this designates a kind of relationship, an achievement among many actors, not all of them human . . . nature is made, but not entirely by humans; it is a co-construction among humans and non-humans."

From this perspective, the world is not separated into subjects (scientists, men, the powerful) and objects (women, animals, "savages"), but instead is composed of subjects-in-interaction, human and nonhuman actors cooperating and struggling with the historical, political, and cultural forces that embed their action. This recasting of the natural world, we maintain, can only proceed within an ethical context that is "grounded in an emotional and spiritual conversation with nonhuman life forms" (Donovan 1990, 375).

living with contradiction

chapter 3

Speaking for Dogs

> A human who truly knows a higher mammal, perhaps a dog or a monkey, and will not be satisfied that these beings experience similarly to himself, is psychologically abnormal and belongs in a psychiatric clinic.
>
> —Konrad Lorenz, in *Der Spiegel* article, 1980

SOCIAL INTERACTION IS a mutual endeavor. It involves taking on the role of the other and, based on the presumptions drawn from this empathic process, adjusting one's behavior to what is seen as the content of the other's "mind." In human-to-human exchanges, judgments about the other's interests, definition of the situation, short- and long-term goals, and so forth are based, most significantly, on what that person *says* about these matters. Language is the privileged vehicle for human interaction (Sheets-Johnstone 1992).

Human social interaction entails, at its simplest, two actors reciprocally oriented toward each other. In his classic discussion of social exchanges, Alfred Schutz (1962, 1970) stresses that interaction involves a presumption of mutually understood motives. That is, as I interact with someone else, I presume that my chosen behavior ("in-order-to motives") is understood by my companion and shapes his or her subsequent behavior (that is, acts as his or her genuine "because-motives"). This exchange is founded on, and oriented by, the shared stock of everyday, commonsense knowledge that constitutes culture (Berger and Luckmann 1966). In short, I presume that what I "know"—that is, what I speak to myself about in the conscious process of constructing my own plans of action—is, at least to some extent, understood by the other and that he or she is similarly involved in the conscious process of constructing and presenting a project of action. This coordinated exchange is possible because the actors involved employ the conventional symbol system of language to talk to themselves and to those with whom they interact. That you and I both are involved in thought and that our exchange is thereby intersubjectively premised (we are mutually aware of the other, mutually motivated to act, mutually able to engage in symbolically mediated communication, and so forth) are key elements of the taken-for-granted reality at the heart of our social encounter.

Speaking For the Other

Difference in power is a key factor shaping the organization of all interactions. The actor who exercises control possesses the ability to determine such central matters as what topic is discussed, when to open and close the exchange, and when conversational interruptions may legitimately occur (Sacks et al. 1974; West and Zimmerman 1977). Another advantage enjoyed by the more powerful interactant is the "right" to express what he or she determines to be what the weaker actor "seems" to be saying, "really means" to say, or would "like" to say. These modes of "interlocution" are typical in settings where the powerful member possesses professionally based or bureaucratically sanctioned office. Psychotherapists (Edelman 1981), advocates in legal proceedings (Buchanan and Brock 1989), and medical doctors (Tannen and Wallat 1983), for example, exercise interactional control in part by routinely expressing the "real" content of the client–patient's internal conversation. In less formal situations, adults commonly speak for children, husbands speak for their wives, employers speak for their employees, and so forth.

Interlocution is, then, a typical feature of human interaction. It is, however, an activity most strikingly revealed in those situations in which one member has a diminished, or nonexistent, capacity to speak effectively or act for him- or herself. Caretakers of Alzheimer's patients, for example, actively involve themselves in making interpretations of the afflicted other's desires and attempt to "normalize" the other's speech and behavior by "filling in gaps," thereby helping to retain some measure of the patient's competence (Fontana and Smith 1989). In so doing, caretakers, like the dog owners and trainers discussed here, participate in socially constructing the mind of the impaired other. Understandings of the likes and dislikes, plans of action, and current emotional state of the Alzheimer's patient are presumed and expressed, based on the able-bodied actor's intimate knowledge of the other gained from their shared history and intimate connections. As Jaber Gubrium (1986, 43) explains:

> As a thing located somewhere behind gesture and expression, mind never presents itself directly to those who take it into account. Hidden as it is, mind must be spoken for. . . . While in theory mind is referenced as a thing, it is articulated and realized by a type of existential labor. Agents are themselves practicing features of mind, even though mind, in its own right, is taken to be a separate and essentially hidden entity.

In a similar fashion, those who routinely interact with retarded persons participate in the collaborative work of communication. Not only does the caretaker "coach" the retarded person in order to get him or her to behave "appropriately" (Kielhofner 1983), but the dominant actor consistently "puts words" in the other's mouth. Pollner and McDonald-Wikler (1985) observe that this sense-making endeavor typically entails the caretaker's "repeating" what the afflicted other "says" and responding to the constructed expression in an ostensibly appropriate fashion. For example, they present the following interchange involving a mother, father, and their severely retarded daughter.

Father: Want to see (your new robe) in the mirror?

Daughter: Gurgling.

Fa: She doesn't like it.

Mother: You don't like the robe? It fits you.

Da: Gurgling.

Mo: What did you say about Daddy?

Da: Mmmmmmmmmmmmmmm, gurgle.

Fa: She thinks it's too cheap. . . . (p. 249; see also Goode 1992; Pollner and Goode 1990)

Interactions of this kind are of considerable sociological interest since they overtly entail the more competent social actor's taking the role of the speechless other, imaginatively putting him- or herself in the perspective of the other party, and giving voice to the other's subjective experience. In short, the more competent interactant works to create the minded 'personhood' of the other and express the contents of this mind in order to construct a basis for grounding interactions that resemble those between ostensibly normal persons (Bogdan and Taylor 1989).

Interactions involving adults and children tend to proceed in similar fashion. Adults make assumptions (often premised on the grossest physical behaviors of the less competent other) about and express the child's presumed thought processes. Below, for example, T. Berry Brazelton, the noted child development expert, describes an infant's cognitive experience—in essence a constructed conversation between the baby and "his" nervous system.

A baby learning to walk will get up and down, up and down, all night and all day. He uses all of his cognitive, motor, and affective energy learning to get up and walk. When he accomplishes that he closes the feedback system—an internal feedback system—which *says,* "You've done it! Isn't that great!" And he walks all day long, *thinking:* "Wow! Wow! Wow! I've done it! It's me!" But his nervous system *says,* "That's great, but it's not good enough. Keep going. You've got to learn to squat. You've got to learn to turn around. You've got to pick up things and walk with them. Keep going." How

Living with Contradiction

does he fuel anything as demanding as that? He has the internal feed-back system, which *says* to him at each step, "You just did it. You're competent...." [Eventually] he will sigh and look around, *as if to say,* "Gosh, I just did it, so I can look around and listen and bring in information from the outside." (1984, 22; emphasis added)

When a child and his or her caretaker are in public settings, adults presume that the child is a kind of "nonperson"; that is, he or she is not regarded as entirely morally responsible. Consequently, the adult member of the dyad typically is held accountable for the child's normative violations and the expectation is that the adult will monitor and control the child's behavior. In this role, the adult often uses breaches of public propriety to illustrate little lessons in appropriate social behavior. Frequently, the adult will direct appropriate verbal responses with such "priming moves" as, "What do you say?" or excuse the derelictions by giving voice to the child's "real" orientation, as in, "He didn't mean to insult you that way." Through these priming and expressive maneuvers, the competent party overtly recognizes the violation and acceptance of public responsibility (Cahill 1987, 1990; cf. Sanders 1990a).

Through these interpretations, assumptions, and empathetically premised interlocutions, those in positions of authority act to construct the personhood of the less competent other (Bogdan and Taylor 1989; Goode 1992, 1994). In this context, being a person is based on a construction of the other as self-conscious, having the ability to understand his or her actions and exercise control over behavior, and able to pursue a line of purposive action (Buchanan and Brock 1989, 159–161). These characteristics of the "person" open the door for the admission of nonhuman actors into the realm of personhood—though the nonhuman animal's self-consciousness is most hotly disputed (Bekoff 1994; Buchanan and Brock 1989, 197–199; Dupre 1990; Griffin 1992; Wemelsfelder 1993).

Typically, those who live with companion animals routinely define them as minded coactors, as virtual persons whose abilities are quantitatively different, but not qualitatively different, from those of humans (Rasmussen et al. 1993). Instead of employing what Bernard

Rollin (1990) refers to as the "common-sense of science," animal caretakers, as practical actors, regard their animals as conscious, purposive, and as engaging in minded behavior (Sanders 1993). In particular, companion dogs (the focus of this discussion) are seen as eminently social creatures with distinct personalities with whom one may develop close and rewarding relationships (Bulcroft et al. 1986; Shapiro 1989). As virtual persons dogs typically are socially incorporated as members of the family (Katcher and Beck 1991) who regularly engage in communicative activities similar to those of the other family members. It is through ongoing interactional experience with the dog that the owner learns to "read" gaze, vocalizations, bodily expressions, and other communicative acts (Baer 1989; McConnell 1991; Ross and McKinney 1992; Serpell 1986; Shapiro 1990b) and, in turn, speaks with the dog in ways that presume that the animal understands what the owner means. As described by Aaron Katcher and Alan Beck (1991, 268), the owner's communicative behavior displays distinct characteristics much like those used in interactions with a child. The owner typically places his or her head close to the animal's and speaks in a quiet voice with a somewhat raised pitch. The rate of speech is slowed and vocalizations tend to be short with phrases rising at the end in a conventional questioning mode.

The animal-person is, however, unable to employ language to respond to the owner's talk or effectively express the content of his or her mind. Like those who have intimate relationships with retarded, ill, or immature humans, owners commonly find themselves in situations in which they feel obliged to translate the dog's point of view, desires, thoughts, or experiences. As the competent language-user, the owner commonly speaks for the animal companion. We turn now to various forms this interlocution takes and some specific settings in which it is practiced.

This discussion is drawn from data collected in two major settings. Sanders spent fourteen months doing participant observation in a large veterinary hospital in the northeast. Some material is drawn from observations of clinical interactions that occurred in this setting. Following the work in the clinic, Sanders was involved in a field study of a guide-dog breeding, training, and placement program. In this setting he became particularly interested in the trainers' interactions with the dogs and their (often ambivalent) understandings of the animals in their charge. Parts of this discussion are based on observations and field conversations recorded in the course of this study.

Modes of "Speaking For"

No matter what the setting in which it occurs, as the "word-user" the human coactor typically gives voice to what he or she understands to be the thoughts or perspective of the dog. In some circumstances, this verbalization is for the speaker's own benefit in that it is central to constructing a dialoguelike exchange with the animal. In other circumstances, for example, in the veterinary setting discussed in the following section, interpreting for the dog or explaining his or her experiences and feelings is intended to promote the interests of the animal. Most basically, then, through empathically determining the feelings, preferences, and thoughts of their dogs and subsequently speaking for their animals, owners actively incorporate their mute companions into the "language community."

In speaking for the dog, the owner demonstrates the intimacy of his or her relationship—the animal other is known so well that the owner can effectively discern what is "on his or her mind." Furthermore, the empathic and verbalizing process is intrinsically pleasurable. It is an integral part of and promotes the intimate relationship between, dog and owner.

It is also through the process of speaking for the dog that the owner actively constructs—both for him- or herself and for others—the identity of the animal (cf., Goode and Waksler 1990). The verbalizations help define the dog and ground its behavior in an understandable context, thereby aiding in constructing the practical interaction chains that constitute collective action.

The interaction of caretakers with their canine companions is commonly quite verbal. Beck and Katcher (1983), for example, found that 80 percent of the veterinary clients they studied talked to their pets "in the same way they talked to people." This communicative activity is typically defined as an authentic conversational exchange in that human caretakers believe that the animal understands what they say and responds appropriately (Beck and Katcher 1983, 44; Cain 1985, 7). Usually the owner speaks slowly and quietly, using short phrases while stretching out words and accenting certain syllables. Katcher and Beck (1991, 268) refer to this "baby-talk" style as "motherese," while Jean Veevers (1985, 20) calls it "doggeral" (cf. Tannen and Wallat 1983).

When speaking to or about a dog or other animal companion owners commonly employ conventional familial labels to incorporate the animal into an everyday, intimate relational context. Veterinary clients routinely presented their relationship with their dogs as familial—they referred to themselves as "Mommy" or "Dad," spoke of their dogs as "the children," and so forth. This convention is so socially powerful that some owners interviewed in the course of the veterinary study—primarily younger couples without children—cited examples in which their own parents spoke of themselves as the dogs' "grandparents." Similarly, veterinarians and support staff often referred to clients as "mommy" and "daddy" when speaking to animal patients in the presence of the owners.

A questioning mode is very common in the verbalizations directed at dogs and other companion animals. The owner's vocal inflection rises at the end of the phrase and then he or she typically pauses to allow the animal to "respond." Owners frequently use this postquestion pause as a "speaking for" opportunity. They "fill in" an appropriate response for the animal, just as humans do for their children. These "priming moves" (Goffman 1971) were observed by Spencer Cahill (1987) in public situations where parents direct "elicitation" questions such as, "What do you say to the nice man?" to their children as part of the socializing process (see also Kaye 1982; West and Zimmerman 1977). In Sanders' observations in the veterinary clinic, he noted that this questioning mode was especially common when owners spoke to their animals. Dogs were frequently asked such direct questions as, "What do you see?" or "Do you want to leave now?" by their human companions.

The question-constructed response style is an example of how owners directly give voice to what they believe their dogs would say if they could use words. In general, this direct, first-person form is common in speaking for. An entry from Sanders' fieldnotes provides an example:

> A young male shepherd with long hair is brought into the exam room by an older couple. The woman does all the talking and even tells us all about what her husband (Frank) does for a living. The husband is generally treated as a nonperson, though he does chime in at times with additions to the information his wife provides. The woman goes on at some length about the dog's long hair and how they hadn't anticipated this when the dog was a puppy. As the talker, the woman does a lot of speaking for the dog (as she does for her husband). The dog lies down with his head on the woman's feet and she says, "Oh, I'm so tired. I just have to lie down here." Later, as the dog is having his nails trimmed, she speaks for the dog in observing, "Oh, I have such nice nails." During much of the time she holds the dog's head tenderly and stares into his eyes.

Veterinarians are accustomed to clients speaking for their animals in the first person and typically find it amusing. As one related, "I come into the exam room and I say, 'Well, how are you doing?' and the woman says, 'Oh Doctor, I'm not feeling all that well.' Later when I'm getting the hypo out, she says, 'Oh Doctor, are you going to give me that shot?' I say, 'No, lady, it's not for you. I don't work on humans.'"

Frequently, in employing the direct manner of speaking for, owners will use the collective "we" convention, as in "We aren't feeling well today." In so doing, the owner clearly demonstrates that he or she, together with the dog, constitute what Erving Goffman (1971) refers to as a "with." The dog-person dyad should be perceived by others as a single acting unit.

Owners also routinely use a somewhat less direct mode of speaking for the animal, typically opening with such statements as, "He doesn't want," or "She feels that." For example:

A chubby middle-aged man has brought in an old black mix-breed dog for her rabies shot. The owner holds the dog on the exam table and constantly strokes her. He tells us about her subjective experience. "She's not in the best of moods. We have a new litter of kittens at home, and they are upsetting her. She hasn't eaten today and she also hasn't peed." [The vet] says, "Well, we'll get this over with fast so that you can get her home and get her filled and emptied." Later we talk about the dog's age and the owner reports on her personal interests. He says, "She still loves to chase sticks. She's just like a puppy."

A subcategory of this type of second-level speaking for is seen when owners employ what Sanders has referred to elsewhere (1990a) as "excusing tactics." When socially more competent actors act in concert with less competent ones, they often feel obliged to provide justifying "accounts" (Hewitt and Stokes 1975; Scott and Lyman 1968) for the others' infractions of social rules. In constructing and offering these "'vocabularies of motive" (Mills 1940) for the other, the ostensibly more responsible (i.e., powerful) member of the dyad, works to repair the damage the violation may have done to the normal flow of social intercourse and the resulting degradation of the responsible member's identity. In human-with-human dyads, these types of surrogate explanations are found when adults are linked with children (Cahill 1987), mentally competent persons are linked with Alzheimer's patients (Fontana and Smith 1989; Gubrium 1986), and psychologically "normal" individuals present the perspectives of associates whose behavior could be interpreted as symptomatic of mental disorder (Lynch 1983).

A final and especially interesting form of speaking for is seen when caretakers engage in what Ann Cain (1983, 79–80) has referred to as "triangling." Essentially, turning the speaking for process around, the speaker presents the virtual voice of the animal to express his or her own orientation, desires, or concerns. The caretaker often uses this mode, like excusing, as a means of protecting social identity in situations where more direct expression could cause embarrassment or discomfort. For example, in the fieldnote

Living with Contradiction

excerpt below, a veterinary client uses the dog to "give orders" to her husband (notice the use of parental references), just as triangling has been observed between people and dogs in public parks (Robbins et al. 1991).

> The owners—a middle-aged married couple—had apparently been involved in some form of argument prior to entering the examination room and the lingering bad feelings between them are fairly obvious. Following the examination and treatment of their dog, the wife asks me where she should go to pay. I tell her where the discharge desk is located. She bends over the dog, turning her back to her husband who is standing at the door, and says, "Why doesn't Daddy take me out to the car while Mommy pays the bill?"

Speaking For Patients and Trainees

The process of "speaking for"—being an interlocutor for the animal—is of central importance in the veterinary situation. In the triadic clinical encounter of veterinary practice, the caretaker and the doctor must work together to define the animal as a "virtual patient"(Gregory and Keto 1991). Since the animal–patient displays only physical signs, the human–client and doctor must construct them as subjectively experienced symptoms (e.g., nausea, pain) in much the same way as in both geriatric and pediatric clinical situations (e.g., Coe and Prendergast 1985; Tannen and Wallat 1983). In the veterinary setting, the client and the veterinarian have differing advantages in their ability to speak for or define the symptoms of the patient. For the client, the animal is usually a familiar companion—there is some level of empathetic bond based on shared history and routinely ongoing interaction (see Shapiro 1990a). Knowing the animal's normal presentation of self, routine behaviors, and unique physical characteristics, the owner is most able to judge divergences from normality. On the other hand, the doctor is trained to judge divergence from *species normality* as opposed to the owner's view of *individual normality.* They can, therefore, act in concert to construct imaginatively the subjective experience of the animal using the evaluative criteria at their disposal. This is often rather problematic in the clinical situation, because the patient typically is quite stressed and what might be seen, especially by the client, as obvious signs of disorder in everyday situations tend to be masked or disappear. Sanders quotes from his fieldnotes:

> [The client] has brought in a mellow male shepherd—Casey—and is concerned that he is limping on his left front leg. She does a bit of "speaking for" in the most typical manner: "He says, I don't like it here. I want to go home." She also expresses her estimates of dog's perceptual experience. "His eyes are getting cloudy. I don't think he sees the way he used to. Well, he can see that cookie when it gets dropped on the floor." [The vet] manipulates the dog's leg joints, first poking at the "wrist" the woman has identified as the sore one. "Well, it doesn't seem to be his wrist. If it was, he would have gone for me or, knowing him, he'd be licking my face. He seems to be having more pain in the elbow here." [He pulls out and rotates the foreleg, and the dog lets out a yelp of pain.] "See."

In this typical example, the client demonstrates her ability to tap into the animal's internal experience (his emotions and visual perception). The veterinarian, in turn, is interested in determining the site of the patient's physical problem and attempts to elicit an externalization (yelp) of the dog's subjective symptom (leg pain).

In addition to speaking for the dog's divergence from normal experience—the factors which prompted them to come to the veterinarian—and the dog's emotional experience while in the medical setting (e.g., "He's nervous here. He doesn't like vets that much."), owners were often observed to speak for their animals by using excusing tactics mentioned above. To a major extent, a dog is an extension of his or her owner's social self (Belk 1988; Sanders 1990b) and, consequently, when the animal's behavior or physical condition diverges from conventional expectations, the owner's image in the eyes of others is potentially degraded. In order to explain these perceived violations, veterinary clients often would verbally assume the role of the pet and from this position explain the infraction. Sanders quotes again from field observations:

> As [the terrier] is getting examined by [the veterinarian], one of the owners stands holding her on the exam table. In order to get to a vein, it turns out to be necessary to shave a small portion of the dog's rather matted foreleg. [The owner] speaks for the dog and offers an excuse for its condition. "I'm kind of matted. They don't take care of me like they used to now that I'm not being shown anymore. I've even been spayed. All I get now is love, but at least they keep me clean—no fleas." [The vet] agrees that there are no fleas. This is an interesting example of "speaking for," since it presents an apology. It is a good example of how owners see the condition of [the] animal as reflecting on their own character.

As a general rule, caretakers' interlocutory actions in the clinical exchanges took one of three general forms. Most commonly, the owner would simply express the animal's experience in the third person. ("He's nervous on slick surfaces, like this floor, and he doesn't like going up stairs. He comes down fine but he has trouble going up. He's much more comfortable on grass.") Sanders noted that owners also often spoke for the dog's experience using the "collective we" ("We aren't going to like this at all."), thereby giving a clear indication of how the person–animal dyad is constructed as a single acting unit.

Another linguistic mode was for owners to employ the direct mode discussed previously. Veterinary clients would often overtly take the role of the animal-other and, from that position, speak back to themselves. Often this mode would incorporate a parental reference, as in the excerpt below:

> A nicely dressed woman comes in with female cocker spaniel she wants debarked. She explains that her regular vet does not do the operation. According to her, this is not because of any ethical concern with the operation, but because he is rather meticulous and the operation is too bloody. She also suspects that the vet doesn't know how to perform the procedure. In the course of the subsequent examination, she speaks for the dog quite directly. Adopting a "sad"

tone of voice, she says, "I'm really nervous here, Mommy. You never leave me in places like this. I want to go home with you."

This can also be observed in a slightly different episode:

> A working-class, middle-aged couple are in the examination room with an eleven-year-old springer spaniel named Queeny. She is a nice dog in very good shape for an old animal. The visit to the clinic is precipitated by the dog's excessive head shaking. During the examination, [the vet] finds minor ear infections and cleans the dog's ears. After one ear is cleaned, the dog hides her face between the body and arm of her owner who is holding her. The man engages in direct "speaking for." "I think I'm going to hide my head here. You aren't going to put that stuff in my ear again." The woman, in turn, does second-level "speaking for." "She thinks that if she can't see you, you can't do anything to her." At another point during the exam, the woman expresses her view of the dog's physical experience when she remarks that the dog is still pretty spry but "doesn't seem to hear that well anymore."

Given the practical concerns of participants in veterinary encounters—to construct a diagnosis and devise appropriate treatments—empathic definition and communication of the animal–patient's subjective experience are clearly important. Similarly, understanding the perspective of the canine-other is of key relevance in training situations where people are engaged in molding the orientations and behaviors of dogs. As in other settings in which humans routinely interact with nonhuman animals, dog trainers display a rather ambivalent perspective on the basic motivations and abilities of their "students." On the one hand, trainers tend to employ (or, at least, profess to believe in) what Wieder (1980) has referred to as "behavioristic operationalism." They define the dog as, in essence, a machine that runs on objectifiable behavioristic principles. Reward, punishment, avoidance, and other behavior-modifying tactics are, from this perspective, the primary tools available for "teaching" the animal to behave in the "appropriate" ways desired by the trainer. On the other hand, dog trainers are practical actors with specific goals. Consequently, they realize that an effective relationship requires that in certain circumstances they must "bracket" their behaviorist assumptions and treat dogs as individuals instead of species representatives. In short, they are frequently called upon to "act as if" individual dogs vary considerably in intelligence (Coren 1994), willingness to please, emotional and physical strength, and so forth. Based on their determinations of individual differences, they shape their interactions with dogs in order to achieve their training goals most effectively (Crist and Lynch 1990; Lenehan 1986). Here, for example, is a passage from fieldnotes recorded early in Sanders' research with guide-dog trainers, which demonstrates the trainer's attempt to define the animal–other so as to structure his relationship with the dog more effectively.

Dick takes the first dog out of the van. We walk for a bit and he tells me about the unique characteristics of the dog we are with. "She gets spooked pretty easy. Like one time we were out training, and this guy just walks out of a door and she got really spooked. Another time a guy was just standing and took out a pack of cigarettes and hit them against his hand, or just looked at his watch or something, and she spooked. She is very sensitive. I have to be careful with her. I can't give too strong a correction or she just cowers." A little later, after we have walked a bit, Dick stops abruptly and looks seriously at the dog. He is obviously deep in thought. He says that he has noticed that the dog is tending to veer to the right and he is trying to decide if it is because of something about her or if it is something he is doing. This is an emerging theme in the research. The trainers understand the dogs' behaviors as a consequence of who/what they are as individuals—with individual characteristics and tendencies—and as a consequence of their experiences—especially their experiences with training. It reflects a kind of nature–nurture distinction. The latter—training interactions—are shaped by the former. How the trainer defines the individual characteristics of the dog determines how he or she will construct the training relationship–interaction with it. The personal characteristics of the trainer also enter into the equation. At one point we are observing and talking about Uvi, a seemingly rather dumb but sweet dog I have seen before, and Dick says, "Yes, they gave Uvi to me at first, but we just didn't get along." He goes on to explain that he defines himself as especially good at training "hard" dogs. He sees Uvi as a "soft" dog, meaning that she is compliant and sensitive.

This rich fieldnote passage reveals a number of key issues. Trainers, of necessity, become adept at reading a dog's "language of action" (Goode 1990, 18). They gauge what the dog is saying about self, others, expectations, goals, and other central elements of the definition of the immediate situation through interpreting the dog's behavior. The note also touches on trainers' most elemental categorization of the dog—other: how the training interaction is structured depends on whether the dog is determined to be hard or soft. In another fieldnote passage, a trainer tells Sanders about the dog he is preparing to work and succinctly summarizes the "hard versus soft" distinction in response to his question.

We park the van in the bank lot and get one of the dogs in harness after releasing her from the crate in back. Mike describes her. "This is Wager. She is a real handful. She is always eager to work and very vocal. She usually goes along just fine, but you can see her holding herself in check." I ask what kinds/categories of dogs there are, remarking that I have heard them use the terms "hard" and "soft." Mike replies, "Those are about it. Soft dogs are sensitive. There are various kinds of soft dogs—people sensitive, traffic sensitive, sound sensitive. A hard dog is just that—a hard dog. It's headstrong, takes a strong hand, is difficult to control. But it is solid and not easily intimidated."

Believing that understanding the individual characteristics of each dog is central to structuring their interactions, the trainers would routinely engage in "speaking for" when they interacted with dogs, conferred with each other about problems, told stories about the day's exploits, or described dogs in response to the questions Sanders asked in the course of field conversations. In another instance:

We get back to the van [after taking one dog on a jaunt around city streets and through a mall], say a few words to the other trainers, take the harness off the first dog, give her some loving, and put her

Living with Contradiction

back in her crate in the van. Judy gets out another dog—a furry male littermate of the first named Uri. Judy describes him for me. "Uri is a good dog. He has a real sense of humor but he's sort of a blockhead, not real smart. He's good because he just does his job. He does what he's been taught. I like dogs like him. The ones I hate to work with are the dogs that are too smart. They take too much initiative. Uri takes correction well. He's not too sensitive. He just shrugs off whatever happens. He just says, 'Oh, okay. If that's what you want, I'll go along with it. No big deal.' He just does what he is told."

The dog trainer's enterprise, then, is an ambivalent one. Although trainers usually speak in behaviorist terms when describing the general activity of dog training or making reference to dogs as a group, they tend to switch modes when describing or dealing with individual canines. One trainer observes:

So your dog gets excited when you pick up your car keys. Everyone says, "Oh, my dog's so smart. He knows when I'm leaving." Of course he does. He's seen you get your keys a thousand times. He simply knows through conditioning—you get the keys, you go. So it's not an intelligent dog, it's just a dog that's observing. So I think there's no doubt that they *can* observe during training and pick up on things that you may not be aware that they're picking up on. But I don't think that they think rationally. It's just their conditioning, knowing from past experiences.

Later in the same conversation, however, this trainer refers to individual dogs as "happy," "willing," and as "displaying different personalities" that the trainer has to take into account. At another point, he remarks:

The dog, for sure, sees no sense in doing [what the trainer requires]. . . . Every day they come to a curb, stop, make a 45-degree turn left. Eventually they say, "Well, why do I have to come to this curb then? Why can't we just go around the corner?"

Clearly, not all trainers feel obliged to think or speak of dogs in such behaviorist terms. For example, William Koehler (1962) emphasizes the dog's "character," Bruce Fogle (1990, ix) observes that "dogs are aware of their own personalities," and Hearne (1987) discusses the dog's "concept of self."

As members of an occupational community, the trainers with whom Sanders worked typically accepted and expressed a behaviorist ideology that cast dogs as "mechanomorphs" that they "subjected" to "conditioning" in order to "implant" specified "responses." However, when confronted with the specific task of teaching individual dogs what Eileen Crist and Michael Lynch (1990) call a "sequential organization of actions," they recognized the necessity of *understanding* the dog as an *individual* and using this understanding to establish a relationship and devise modes of interacting that were *meaningful* to that dog. The practicalities of their work require them to think and act in terms of the dog's unique personality, emotional experience, and thought processes (mind).

Exchanges between people and animals are central to the ongoing flow of contemporary social life. As is the case of interactions with other alingual actors (Goode 1990; Gubrium 1986; Pollner and McDonald-Wikler 1985), the understandings we derive in our encounters with companion animals are found largely in our connections to them built up over the course of the routine, practical, and empathetic interactions that make up our shared biographies (Shapiro 1989). In other words, through understanding the bodies and behaviors of companion animals we actively construct a view of their minds. This is especially so with canine companions in that, of all pet animals, dogs are most likely to be defined by their human coactors as possessing minds that operate in many ways like our own (Eddy et al. 1993; Rasmussen et al. 1993). A natural and useful consequence of our socially constructed understanding of the dog's mind is that we regularly find ourselves in situations that make it necessary, convenient, or intrinsically rewarding for us to give voice to what we "know" to be the dog's subjective experience.

Whether this construction of the dog's mind is "true" in some objective sense—that is, whether the animal is "actually" thinking, planning, intending, or feeling in the ways we present—is not the central issue. It may be, of course, that in speaking for the dogs with whom we share our daily lives we are simply, as Eugene Rochberg-Halton (1985) presumes, constructing "dialogues with the self." But, as Alfred Schutz (1970) and other phenomenologists emphasize, this may also be true of our interactions with human cointeractants. Even for language-users, intersubjectivity is a notoriously presumptive endeavor. The accuracy of our understandings of the other—human or nonhuman—is grounded primarily on our *sense* of his or her body and behavior. The validity of this understanding is confirmed or denied by its practical outcomes. The "truth" of our perceptions and expressions of the other's orientation derives from whether these understandings work to establish communication (Bright 1990) and sustain a viable and mutually rewarding flow of interaction.

Social scientists tend to take a linguacentric stance in their attempts to understand social interaction and the presumed "inner dialogue" that constitutes "mind." This privileging of language frequently is used to deny that nonhuman animals engage in minded behavior. We would maintain, as do the cognitive ethologists and many other analysts of animal behavior, that language is overrated as the primary vehicle of cognition and coordinated social interaction. As human mental and physical "disabilities" are matters of social construction rather than determinations of the actual abilities of the other (Higgins 1992), so the view of dogs and other animal companions as mindless and uncommunicative is a social construction. The presumption that language is essential for an actor to experience empathy with others, construct viable lines of collective action, and engage in cognitive activities is, at best, debatable. As Donald Ellis (1991, 217) observes in his critique of poststructuralism's focus on language:

> Thought and cognition exist in the absence of natural language. . . .
> Thought exists in the absence of oral language and it is even possible to make the argument that language and thought are independent. Experiments that compare the problem solving of deaf children who have no verbal symbol system to that of hearing

children with sophisticated language conclude that both groups solve problems with equal effectiveness and use identical strategies. . . . Deaf children with no language (including no sign language) still possess and represent information in some mode other than a linguistic one. . . . *Interaction is more necessary for thinking and cognition than language.* (Emphasis added; see also Tester 1991, 1–16)

Conventionally, those enamored of "objective" science have denigrated owners' understandings and articulations of their animals' subjectivities as grounded in "folk psychology," the simplistic and unscientific view that our own behaviors and those of our cointeractants are shaped by such commonsense constructs as "desire" or "belief " (see Beer 1991). When these folk psychological concepts are applied specifically to the subjective experience and behavior of nonhuman animals, this point of view is further derogated as representing anthropomorphism. Around this issue a vigorous and often rancorous debate revolves (see, for example, Eddy et al. 1993; Fisher 1991; Kennedy 1992; Stebbins 1993). Behaviorists and many ethologists roundly condemn anthropomorphic descriptions while everyday pet owners and most members of the animal rights community routinely make use of anthropomorphism as a dominant vehicle for making sense of animal behavior.

The middle ground in this debate is mapped out by those who identify with what has come to be known as "cognitive ethology" (Griffin 1992; Ristau 1991; Wilder 1990). This orientation, in essence, views anthropomorphism as a useful heuristic device. In advocating what he calls "critical anthropomorphism," Gordon Burghardt (1991) maintains that building a systematic understanding of animal behavior is the prime goal. In achieving this goal, such tools as introspection, reasoning by analogy, interpretive analysis, and intuition should not be discarded simply because they are not currently in favor in certain scientific circles. In this regard, Timothy Eddy and his associates (1993) as well as James Serpell (1986) emphasize the evolutionary roots of anthropomorphism in the necessity of coordinating social behavior and the practical utility of employing an understanding of one's own perspectives, emotions, thoughts, and intentions as a basis for understanding the situational definitions and plans of action constructed by cointeractants, be they human or nonhuman. The Cartesian construction of nonhuman animals as behavioristic machines (the dominant view that Hearne [1987] derogatorily refers to as "mechanomorphism"), in contrast, yields an impoverished and impractical view of animal behavior. As Hearne notes:

> To the extent that the behaviorist manages to deny any belief in the dog's potential for believing, intending, meaning, etc., there will be no flow of intention, meaning, believing, hoping going on. The dog may try to respond to the behaviorist, but the behaviorist won't respond to the dog's response. . . . The behaviorist's dog will not only seem stupid, she will be stupid. (p. 58)

At the same time, the behaviorist perspective allows humans to maintain the psychological distance necessary to exploit animals ruthlessly, untroubled by feelings of guilt while still retaining a view of humans as a qualitatively unique category of being.

On the other hand, the natural attitude in which companion animals and other nonhuman actors are regarded as minded, emotional, and intentional—and whose orientations and interests can be spoken for with some degree of validity—has the practical utility of allowing the construction of effective and mutually rewarding patterns of social interaction. Additionally, this perspective casts nonhuman animals as worthy of moral concern (Rowan 1991).

Human exchanges with nonhuman animals involve knowing, relating to, shaping interactions with, and responding to the interactional moves of the animal–other. Systematically studying these social exchanges provides us with what Donald Griffin (1976) refers to as a major "window to animal mind." The usual stance of empathetic pet caretakers and practical dog trainers, as demonstrated in their experientially acquired ability to comprehend and give voice to the mind and experience of their animal companions, offers a worthy model to social scientists devoted to examining and understanding interspecies interactions.

chapter 4

The Institutional Self of
Shelter Workers

> You will want to care for the animals, but will have to kill some of
> them . . . when you don't want to. It seems so bad, but we'll make it
> good in your head.
>
> —Shelter manager, in Euthanasia Workshop

SHORING UP the normative order in any culture are attitudes and
institutions that provide ways out of the culture's contradictions by
supplying myths to bridge them and techniques to assuage troubled
feelings. While researchers interested in contradictory attitudes toward different human groups have long since demonstrated the role
of institutions in the perpetuation of racism, a similar focus has been
strikingly absent in discussions of contradictory attitudes toward animals. It may be useful, then, to begin to ask how institutions can
transform ordinary people, who themselves may own dogs or cats as
pets, into workers who can kill members of these same species.

Humane and scientific institutions, for example, must teach
newcomers in shelters and laboratories to suspend their prior,
everyday, or commonsense thinking about the use and meaning of
animals and adopt a different set of assumptions that may be in-

consistent with their original views about animals. These assumptions are not themselves proved but rather structure and form the field upon which animals are used by institutions. Typically, the assumptions are transmitted to nascent practitioners of a discipline, along with relevant empirical facts and skills, as indisputable truths, not as debatable points. Newcomers must accept the premise of the institution—often that it is necessary to kill animals—and get on with the business of the institution. But exactly how do they get on with this business?

In addition to learning to think differently about the proper fate of animals in institutions, workers must learn to feel differently about them in that situation. Newcomers may experience uncomfortable feelings even if they accept the premise of the institution on an intellectual level. Although institutions will, no doubt, equip newcomers with rules and resources for managing unwanted emotions, researchers have not examined how such emotion-management strategies actually work and the extent to which they can eliminate uncomfortable feelings. In the absence of such research, it is generally assumed that newcomers learn ways to distance themselves from their acts and lessen their feelings of guilt. These tactics are thought to prevent any attachment to and empathy for animals (Schleifer 1985) and to make killing "a reflex, virtually devoid of emotional content" (Serpell 1986, 152).

To examine these assumptions, Arluke conducted ethnographic research over a seven-month period in a "kill-shelter" serving a major metropolitan area. Such a case study seemed warranted, given the sensitivity of the topic under study. He became immersed in this setting, spending more than a hundred hours in direct observation of all facets of shelter work and life, including the euthanizing of animals and the training of workers to do it. Also, he conducted interviews with the entire staff of sixteen people, many formally and at length on tape, about euthanasia and related aspects of shelter work. These interviews were open-ended and semistructured, allowing workers to explore and elaborate on their thinking and feeling without being unduly constrained by the limits of a formal questionnaire.

His findings suggest that learning to cope with the uncomfortable feelings provoked by euthanasia in shelters is a complex social process. Feelings such as attachment, empathy, and loss were not eliminated but instead came to serve as coping devices that enabled workers to maintain a sense of themselves as people who liked and cared for animals. This was their new, institutional self, and it served them well, enabling them to do their work with a minimum of conflict. Yet, far from being completely detached from their charges, all workers became uneasy at times, although for different reasons, when their everyday noninstitutional identities emerged at work.

The Newcomers' Problem

Euthanasia posed a substantial emotional challenge to most novice shelter workers. People seeking work at the shelter typically regarded themselves as "animal people" or "animal lovers" and recounted life-long histories of keeping pets, collecting animals, nursing strays, and working in zoos, pet stores, veterinary practices, and even animal research laboratories. They came wanting to "work with animals" and expecting to spend much of their time in hands-on contact with animals in a setting where others shared the same high priority they placed on human–animal interaction. The prospect of having to kill animals seemed incompatible with this self-conception.

When first applying for their jobs, some shelter workers did not even know that euthanasia was practiced at the shelter. To address this possible misconception, applicants were asked how they would feel when it was their turn to euthanize. Most reported that they did not really think through this question at the time, but simply replied that they thought it was "okay" in order to get the job. One worker, for instance, said she "just put this thought out of my mind," while another worker said that she had hoped to "sleaze out" of doing it. Many said that having to perform euthanasia did not fully sink in until they "looked the animal in its eyes." Clearly, newcomers were emotionally unprepared to actually euthanize animals.

Once on the job, newcomers quickly formed strong attachments to particular animals. In fact, it was customary to caution newcomers against adopting animals right away, but several factors encouraged these attachments. Many of the animals were healthy and appealing, and the animals sometimes initiated interaction with workers. Newcomers also saw the senior staff interacting with animals in a petlike fashion. Shelter animals, for example, were all named, and everyone used these names when referring to the animals. Although newcomers followed suit, they did not realize that more experienced workers could interact this way with animals without becoming attached to them. Moreover, newcomers found that their work required them to know the individual personalities of shelter animals in order to make sound decisions regarding adoption and euthanasia, but this knowledge readily fostered attachments. Not surprisingly, the prospect of having to kill animals to whom they had become attached was a major concern for newcomers. This anticipated relationship with shelter animals made newcomers agonize when they imagined selecting animals for euthanasia and seeing "trusting looks" on the faces of those to be killed. They also worried about having to cope with the "losses" they expected to feel after killing these animals.

Further aggravating the novices' trepidation was the fact that they had to kill animals for no higher purpose. Many felt grieved and frustrated by what they saw as the "senseless" killing of healthy animals. Several newcomers flinched at the shelter's willingness to kill animals if suitable homes were not found instead of "fostering out" the animals. In their opinion, putting animals in less than "ideal" homes for a few years was better than death.

The clash between the feelings of newcomers for shelter animals and the institution's practice of euthanasia led newcomers to experience a caring–killing "paradox." On the one hand, they tried to understand and embrace the institutional rationale for euthanasia, but on the other hand, they wanted to nurture and tend to shelter animals. Doing both seemed impossible to many newcomers. Acceptance of the need for euthanasia did not remove the apprehension that workers felt about having to kill animals themselves or to be part of this process. Their everyday selves were still paramount and made them feel for shelter animals as they might toward their own pets—the thought of killing them was troubling. They even feared getting to the point where they would no longer be upset over killing animals, commonly asking those more senior, "Do you still care?" or, "Doesn't it still bother you?"

Experienced shelter workers acknowledged the "paradox" of the newcomers, reassuring them that:

> There is a terrible paradox in what you will have to do—you will want to care for the animals, but will have to kill some of them. It is a painful process of killing animals when you don't want to. It seems so bad, but we'll make it good in your head. You will find yourself in a complex emotional state. Euthanizing is not just technical skills. You have to believe it is right to make it matter-of-fact.

Emotion-Management Strategies

How did shelter workers manage their uncomfortable feelings? Workers learned different emotion-management strategies to distance themselves enough to kill, but not so far as to abandon a sense of themselves as animal people. These strategies enabled workers at least to hold in abeyance their prior, everyday sensibilities regarding animals and to apply a different emotional perspective while at the shelter.

Virtual Pets

New workers' initial failure to distinguish shelter animals from their own pets could put them in emotionally jarring situations, especially when animals were euthanized. Most of them, however, soon came to see shelter animals as "virtual pets"—lying somewhere between the categories of pet and object. Workers could maintain a safe distance from animals in such a liminal status, while not entirely detaching themselves from them.

One way they accomplished this shift was to lessen the intensity of their emotional attachments to individual animals. Almost as a rite of passage, newcomers were soon burned by the euthanasia of a favorite animal and distraught over the loss. They also heard cautionary tales about workers who were very upset by the loss of animals to whom they had grown "too close" as well as workers whose "excessive" or "crazy" attachments resulted in harm to the animals—such as the woman who was fired after she released all the dogs from the shelter because she could no longer stand to see them caged or put to death. Newcomers soon began consciously to withhold affection. As one worker observed, "I don't let myself get that attached to any of them."

On the other hand, certain mottoes or ideals were part of the shelter culture, underscoring the importance of not distancing themselves completely from their charges or becoming desensitized to euthanasia. One worker told Arluke that you "learn to turn your feelings off when you do this work, but you can't completely. They say if you can, you shouldn't be on the job." Another worker noted, "If you get to the point where killing doesn't bother you, then you shouldn't be working here."

While they stopped themselves from "loving" individual shelter animals because of their likely fate, workers learned that they could become more safely attached by maintaining a generalized caring feeling for shelter animals as a group. As the new workers became more seasoned, individual bonding became less frequent, interest in adopting subsided, and a sense emerged of corporate attachment to shelter animals as a population of refugees rather than as individual pets.

Workers also came to see shelter animals differently from ordinary pets by assuming professional roles with their charges. One role was that of "caretaker" rather than pet owner. As a worker remarked, "You don't set yourself up by seeing them as pets. You'd kill yourself; I'd cut my wrists. I'm a caretaker, so I make them feel better while they are here. They won't be forgotten so quickly. I feel I get to know them. I'm their last hope." Comparing her own pet to shelter animals, another worker noted, "No bell goes off in your head with your own pet as it would with a shelter animal, where the bell says you can't love this animal because you have to euthanize it." If not caretakers, they could become social workers trying to place these animals in the homes of other people.

New workers came to view their charges as having a kind of market value within the larger population of shelter animals. Workers were not to use their own preferences and values to judge animals. Rather, they were to be assessed in terms of their competitive attractiveness to potential adopters. This view was nowhere more apparent than in the selection of healthy and well-behaved animals to be euthanized in order to make room for incoming animals. An experienced shelter worker described these "tough choices" and the difficulty newcomers had in viewing animals this way:

> When you go through and "pull"—that's when you have to make some real tough choices. If they've all been here an equal amount of time, then, if you've got eighteen cages and six are filled with black cats, and you have a variety in here waiting for cages, you're going to pull the black ones so you can have more of a variety. It's hard for a new employee to understand that I'm going to pull a black cat to make room for a white one. After they've been here through a cat season, they know exactly what I'm doing, and you don't have to say anything when you have old staff around you.

In addition, newcomers learned to think about spending money for the medical care of shelter animals differently from the way they would for their own pets. Although an occasional animal might receive some medical attention, many animals were killed because it was not considered economically feasible to treat them even though they had reversible problems and the cost might be negligible. For example, while two newcomers observed the euthanizing of several kittens, an experienced worker pointed to a virus in their mouths as the reason for their being killed. One newcomer asked why the kittens could not be treated medically so they could be put up for adoption. The reply was that the virus could be treated, but "given the volume, it's not economical to treat them."

Keeping shelter mascots further helped workers separate pets from their charges, with mascots serving as surrogate pets for the rest of the shelter's animals. Cats and dogs were occasionally singled out to become group mascots, the former because workers took a special interest in them, the latter because workers hoped to increase their adoptability by improving their behavior.

Unlike other shelter animals, mascots were permitted to run free in areas reserved for workers, such as their private office and the front desk, where workers played with them and talked about them. More significantly, mascots were never euthanized; either they remained indefinitely in the shelter or went home as someone's pet. Although most shelter workers interacted with the mascots as though they were pets, one shelter worker, very like an owner, often took a special interest in a mascot and let it be known that she would eventually adopt the animal if a good home could not be found. Some of the workers' behavior toward these mascots was in clear contrast to the way they acted toward regular shelter animals. For one example, a mascot cat was found to have a stomach ailment requiring expensive surgery. Under normal circumstances, this animal would have been killed, but one of the workers used her own money to pay for the operation.

Using the Animal

By taking the feelings of animals into account, workers distracted themselves from their own discomfort with euthanizing. They tried to make this experience as "good" as possible for the animals and, in so doing, felt better themselves. Some workers, in fact, openly admitted that "it makes me feel better making it [euthanasia] better for the animal." Even more seasoned workers were more at ease with euthanasia if they focused on making animals feel secure and calm as they were killed. A worker with twenty years' experience remarked that "it still bothers you after you're here for a long time, but not as much. Compassion and tenderness are there when I euthanize, so it doesn't eat away at me."

One way workers supported the animals was to empathize with them in order to figure out how to reduce each animal's stress during euthanasia. By seeing things from the animal's perspective, workers sought to make the process of dying "peaceful and easy." As a worker pointed out, "You make the animal comfortable and happy and secure, so when the time to euthanize comes, it will not be under stress and scared—the dog will lick your face, the cats will purr." In the words of another worker, "They get more love in the last few seconds than they ever did." Workers were encouraged to "think of all the little things that might stress the animal—if you sense that some are afraid of men, then keep men away." Acting on the same principle, another worker decided not to have cats and dogs in the euthanasia room at the same time. Actual observation of euthanasia confirmed the workers' consideration of the animals' states of mind. When a cat and her kittens had to be euthanized, the mother was killed first to spare her sensing that her kittens were dying. And in another instance, a worker refused to be interviewed during euthanasia because she felt that our talking made the animals more anxious.

Another way that taking animals' feelings into consideration helped workers was by concentrating on the methodology of killing and becoming technically proficient at it. By focusing on the technique of killing—and not on why it needed to be done or how they felt about doing it—workers could reassure themselves that they were making death quick and painless for animals.

Workers known as "shooters" injected the euthanasia drug and were told to "focus not on the euthanasia, but on the needle. Concentrate on technical skills if you are the shooter." Those who merely held animals steady during injection, known as "holders," were taught to view their participation as a technical act as opposed to a demonstration of affection. In the words of a worker, "The holder is the one who controls the dog. You have your arm around her. You're the one who has got a hold of that vein. When they get the blood in the syringe, you let go. But you have to hold that dog and try and keep him steady and not let him pull away. That's my job." Senior workers reacted strongly against bad killing technique in shooting or holding. As one noted, "I get really pissed off if someone blows a vein if it is due to an improper hold."

Since the act of euthanasia was regarded more as a technical rather than a moral or emotional issue, it was not surprising that workers could acquire reputations within the shelter for being "good shots," and animals came to be seen as either easy or hard "put downs"—a division reflecting technical difficulty and increased physical discomfort for animals. If the animal was a "hard put down," workers became all the more absorbed in the mechanics of euthanasia, knowing that the sharpness of their technical skills would affect the extent of an animal's distress. A worker illustrated the situation thus:

> Old dogs, the ones that should have been euthanized two years ago, those are hard to put down because they're so old. You know, their veins are just not pumping as fast as they should. You can inject it and the vein can blow up. It's an old vein. You have to go real slow. Sometimes they just get kind of clogged. It's really tough. It's hard to get the veins on them sometimes. You feel badly about that because sometimes you have to . . . use all four legs before you get a good one.

Workers could also take the animals' welfare into consideration, rather than focus on their own feelings, by seeing their death as the alleviation of suffering. This was easy to do with animals that were very sick or old—known as "automatic kills"—but it was much harder to see suffering in "healthy and happy" animals. They, too, had to be seen as having lives not worth living. Workers were aware that the breadth of their definition of suffering made euthanasia easier for them. One worker acknowledged, "Sometimes you want to find any reason [to euthanize], like it has a runny nose," because killing was harder to do without a reason. Newcomers often flinched at what was deemed sufficient medical or psychological reason to euthanize an animal, as did veterinary technicians working in the adjoining animal hospital who sometimes sarcastically said to shelter workers or their animals, "If you cough, they will kill you. If you sneeze, they will kill you."

Workers also learned to see euthanasia as a way to prevent suffering; that is, it was thought better to euthanize healthy strays than to let them "suffer" on the streets. One senior worker told newcomers:

> I'd rather kill than see suffering. I've seen dogs hung in alleys, cats with firecrackers in their mouths or caught in car fan belts. This helps me to cope with euthanizing—to prevent this suffering through euthanasia. Am I sick if I can do this for fifteen years? No. I still cry when I see a sick pigeon on the streets, but I believe in what I am doing.

Once in the shelter, healthy strays, along with abandoned and surrendered animals, were also thought better dead than "fostered out." A worker noted, "I'd rather kill it now then let it live three years and die a horrible death. No life is better than a temporary life." Even having a potential adopter was not enough.

> Finding an appropriate home for the animal is the only way the animal is going to get out of here alive. The inappropriate home prolongs the suffering, prolongs the agony, prolongs the neglect, prolongs the abuse of an animal. The animal was abused or neglected in the first place or it wouldn't be here.

This thinking was a problem for newcomers who believed that almost any home, even if temporary, was better than killing animals. Particularly troubling were those people denied adoption even though their resources and attitudes seemed acceptable to workers. For instance, some potential adopters were rejected because shelter staff thought that they would not be home enough, even though by all other standards they seemed likely to become good owners. In one case, a veterinary hospital technician wanted to adopt a four-month-old puppy but was rejected because she had full-time employment. Although she retorted that she had a roommate who was at home most of the time, her request was still denied.

But newcomers soon learned to scrutinize potential adopters carefully by screening them for certain warning flags, such as an unwillingness to spay or neuter animals, keep them fenced in or leashed, spend enough time with them, or obtain a landlord's approval. Most workers came to see certain groups of people as risky adopters requiring even greater scrutiny before approval. For some workers, this meant welfare recipients because they might not have enough money to care for animals, Latinos because they were unwilling to spay or neuter, or police officers because they might be too rough with animals.

Although workers accepted the applications of most potential owners, they did reject some. Even in their acceptances, they reaffirmed their concern for suffering and their desire to find perfect homes; they did so even more strongly with their rejections, admonishing those turned down for whatever their presumed deficiencies were. Occasionally, rejected applicants became irate and made angry comments such as, "You'd rather kill it then give it to me!" These moments were uncomfortable for newcomers to experience, since, to some extent, they shared the rejected applicant's sentiment—any home was better than death. More experienced workers would try to cool off the applicant but they also reminded newcomers that some homes were worse than death. In one encounter, the shelter manager told the rejected applicant—but for all to hear—"It is my intention to find a good home where the animal's needs can be met."

Resisting and Avoiding Euthanasia

New workers, in particular, sometimes managed their discomfort with euthanasia by trying to prevent or delay the death of animals. Although there were generally understood euthanasia guidelines, they were rather vague, and workers could exert mild pressure to make exceptions to these rules. Certainly, not all animals scheduled, or "pink-slipped," to be killed were "automatic kills." As a worker noted, "If a twelve-year-old stray with hip dysplasia comes in, yes, you know as soon as it walks in the door that at the end of the stray holding period it's going to be euthanized, but not all of them are like this." Another worker described such an instance:

> Four weeks is really young. Five weeks, you're really pushing it. Six weeks, we can take it, but it depends on its overall health and condition. But sometimes we'll keep one or two younger ones,

depending on the animal itself. We just had an animal last week—it was a dachshund. She is a really nice and friendly dog. In this case, we just decided to keep her.

Sometimes a worker took a special liking to a particular animal, which was to be euthanized because the cage was needed for new animals, or it was too young, too old, somewhat sick, or a behavior problem. The worker might let it be known among peers that he or she was very attached to the animal, or go directly to the person making the euthanasia selection with a plea to delay the animal's death in the hopes of adoption. One worker, for instance, who had a favorite cat that was scheduled to be euthanized, successfully blocked its killing, at least for a while, by personally taking financial responsibility for its shelter costs.

Workers had to oppose euthanasia, however, in a way that did not cause too much conflict for decision makers. Workers could not object repeatedly to euthanasia or oppose it too aggressively without making the selector feel very uncomfortable. One worker elaborated on what happened to her.

> There was one technician—Marie—who used to make me feel guilty. I have to make room for new animals because we have so few cages. I must decide which old ones to kill to make room for new ones. Marie would get upset when I would choose certain cats to be killed. She would come to me with her runny, snotty nose, complaining that certain cats were picked to be killed. This made me feel guilty.

More experienced workers saw these "objections" as emotions clouding "reality," as one senior worker explained.

> Sometimes staff object because they think an animal should have longer. They'll say, "Why does this one have to go?" But a lot of it is emotion getting in the way of the reality of what an animal shelter is. I know I regret having to euthanize particular animals, but I also know there's always a reason, whether it has been here too long—dogs go cage crazy or suffer kennel stress or we need their cage to make room for incoming animals. So there's always a reason.

If their opposition was in vain, workers could still avoid the discomfort of doing it themselves. One worker described the strategy this way:

> There's not an animal I'm not attached to here, but there's a cat here now that I like a lot. There's a good chance that she'll be euthanized. She's got a heart murmur, I guess. It's a mild one, but . . . any type of a heart murmur with a cat is bad. She's also got a lump right here. They've already tested her for leukemia and it's negative, so they are testing her for something else. But she's just got an adorable face and everything else with her is fine. I like her personality. But I have two cats at home. I can't have a third. I won't be around when they euthanize her. I'll let somebody else do it. I would rather it be done when I'm not here.

Although workers could be exempted from killing animals with whom they had closely bonded, others had a strong feeling that they should be there for the animal's sake. They could then indicate to the others that they did not want to be the "shooter" and would be the "holder" instead, thus allowing themselves to feel more removed from the actual killing. A staffer noted:

> Especially if it's one I like a lot, I would rather be the one holding instead of injecting. If you don't want to inject, you just back up and somebody else does it. Everybody here does that. I just look at it, I don't want to be the one to do it. Even though people say that holding is the harder of the two, I would look at it as, well, I am the one who is doing this. And sometimes, I don't want to be the one to do it.

Customizing the division of labor of euthanasia to fit their own emotional limits, other workers preferred not to do the holding. One worker explained his choice:

> One of the ways that I detach myself from euthanasia is that I do the shooting rather than the holding so that I don't feel the animal dying. I'm concentrating on the technical skill behind the actual injection. And with a dog, you literally feel the animal's life go out of it in your arms, instead of giving the injection and letting it drop.

Using the Owner

Shelter workers could also displace some of their own discomfort with euthanasia into anger at and frustration with pet owners. Rather than questioning the morality of their own acts and feeling guilty, workers came to see owners, and not themselves, as wronging the animals. As workers transferred the blame for killing animals to the public, they then concentrated their energies on educating and changing public attitudes toward pets and making successful adoptions through the shelter.

The public was seen as treating animals as "property to be thrown away like trash" rather than as having their own intrinsic value. One worker bemoaned, "A lot of people who want to leave their pets have bullshit reasons for this—like they just bought new furniture for their living room and their cat sheds all over it." This lack of commitment to pets resulted in many of these surrendered animals being euthanized because they were not adoptable and/or space was scarce. Speaking about these owners, one worker candidly acknowledged, "I would love to be rude once to some of these people who come in. I'd like to say to these people—'cut this bullsic out!'" Another worker concluded, "You do want to strangle these people."

Even pet owners who did not surrender their animals to the shelter became tainted in the eyes of workers who saw many of them as negligent or irresponsible. A common charge against owners was that they allowed their pets to run free and get hurt, lost, or stolen. One senior worker admitted, "A bias does get built in. We're called if a cat gets caught in a fan belt. We're the ones that have to scrape cats off the streets."

Owners were also seen as selfish and misguided when it came to their pets for thoughtlessly allowing them to breed, instead of spaying or neutering them. Workers often repeated the shelter's pithy wish: "Parents will let their pets have puppies or kittens so they can show their children the miracle of birth—well, maybe they should come in here to see the miracle of death!" Workers could be heard among themselves denouncing the public's "irresponsibility" toward breeding and the deaths that such an attitude caused. A worker explained, "The only reason why it has been killed is that no one took the time to be a responsible pet owner. They felt the cat deserved to run free, or they didn't want to pay the money to have it spayed or neutered, or that she should have one litter. Well great, what are you to do with her six offspring?"

Owners who professed great love and affection for their pets sometimes came across in the shelter environment as cruel to them. These were owners who let their animals suffer because they could not bear to kill them. A worker described them:

> I'll get a twenty-two-year-old cat. And their owner is crying out there. I tell her, "You know, twenty-two years is great. You have nothing to be ashamed of. Nothing." But you get some others that come in and they [the animals] look absolutely like shit. You feel like taking hold of them and saying, "What the hell are you doing? He should have been put to sleep two years ago!"

According to shelter workers, owners should have suffered pangs of conscience about their treatment of animals, but did not. Some owners seemed not to want their pets, and this shocked workers, as one of them noted, "You'd be surprised at how many people come right out and say they don't want it anymore. They are usually the ones who call us to pick it up, otherwise they'll dump it on the street. And of course, we're going to come get it. I feel like saying, 'It's your conscience, not mine, go ahead, do it.' Of course, I don't do that." Many surrenderers, in the eyes of shelter workers, just did not care whether their animals lived or died. At the same time that surrenderers were seen as conscienceless, shelter workers were afforded the opportunity to reaffirm their own dedication to and feelings for animals. A worker commented:

> Some surrenderers take them back after we tell them we can't guarantee placement. Most say, "Well that's fine." Like the owner of this cat, he called this morning and he said, "I've got to get rid of it, I'm allergic to it." Of course, he didn't seem at all bothered. He goes, "That's fine." Or somebody is going to surrender a pet because they're moving, well, if it was me, and I'm sure quite a few other people here feel the same way, I'd look for a place where pets

were allowed. People are just looking out for themselves and not anything else.

In the opinion of the experienced workers, it was important for newcomers to learn not to assume the "guilt" that owners should have felt. To do this, they had to see owners as the real killers of shelter animals. As one worker put it, "People think we are murderers, but they are the ones that have put us in this position. We are morally offended by the fact that we have to carry out an execution that we didn't necessarily order." One senior shelter worker recounted vividly how she came to terms with guilt.

> Every night I had a recurring dream that I died, and I was standing in line to go to heaven. And St. Peter says to me, "I know you, you're the one that killed all those little animals." And I'd sit up in the bed in a cold sweat. Finally, when I realized it wasn't my fault, my dreams changed. After St. Peter said, "I know you, you're the one that killed all those little animals," I turned to one of the 999,000 people behind me and said, "I know you, you made me kill all these animals." You grow into the fact that you are the executioner, but you weren't judge and jury.

Shelter workers redirected their emotions and resources into changing public attitudes about pets in order to curtail the never-ending flow of animals—often called a "flood"—that always far exceeded the possibilities for adoption. Overwhelmed by this problem, workers wanted to do something about it other than killing animals. By putting their efforts into adoption or public education, workers felt they were making a dent in the overpopulation problem instead of feeling hopeless about it. For many, combating pet overpopulation became a mission. Rather than chewing over the morality of their own participation in euthanasia, they became part of a serious campaign—often described as a "battle"—in defense of helpless animals and against the formidable foe of the pet owner.

Owners were not always objects of blame. Successful adoptions helped to accentuate the positive in a setting where there were few opportunities for the staff to feel good about what they were doing. Finding homes for animals came close to the original motivation that brought many workers to the shelter seeking employment. One worker commented, "For every one euthanized, you have to think about the one placed, or the one case where you placed it in a perfect family." Another worker said that "you get a good feeling when you see an empty cage." When she saw an empty cage, she did not think that it was empty because an animal had just been killed, but rather because an animal had just been adopted. Indeed, when the cage of someone's "favorite" was empty, out of self-protection, workers did not ask what happened so that they could assume that the animal had been adopted. They talked about how all of their animals were "either PWP or PWG—placed with people or placed with God." Shelter workers felt particularly gratified when they heard from people who had satisfactorily adopted animals. Some owners came to the shelter and talked informally with workers; others wrote letters of thanks for their pets. Beside taping these letters on the walls for all to see, snapshots of adopters and their animals were mounted in the lobby.

Dealing with Outsiders

For workers to manage their emotions successfully, they also had to learn to refrain from asking hard ethical questions. This was easier to do within the confines of the shelter than on the outside. Many reported feeling bad when outsiders challenged them about the morality of euthanasia. Workers dealt with these unwanted feelings in two ways.

Outside work, they could try to avoid the kinds of contacts that gave rise to difficult questions and unwanted emotions. Workers claimed that roommates, spouses, family members, and strangers sometimes saw them as "villains" or "murderers" and made them feel "guilty." As one worker put it, "You expect your spouse, your parents, your sister, your brother, or your significant other to understand. And they don't. And your friends don't. People make stupid remarks like, 'Gee, I would never do your job because I love animals too much.'" Workers claimed that they had become "paranoid" about being asked if they killed animals, waiting for questions such as, "How can you kill them if you care about animals so much?" One worker claimed that these questions and comments "make me feel like I've done something wrong." Another said, "So what does it mean—I don't love animals?" If workers were not explicitly criticized or misunderstood, they still encountered people who made them feel reluctant to talk about their work. One worker noted, "I'm proud that I'm a 90 percent shot and that I'm not putting the animals through stress, but people don't want to hear this."

In anticipation of these negative reactions, many workers hesitated to divulge what they did for a living. One worker, for example, said that she had learned to tell people that she "drives an animal ambulance." When some workers revealed that they did euthanasia, they often presented arguments to support their caring for animals and the need for euthanasia. As one worker reported, "I throw numbers at them, like the fact that we get twelve thousand animals a year but can only place two thousand." While concealing their workplace or educating others about animal overpopulation were by far the most common strategies used with outsiders, some workers would occasionally take a blunter approach by way of sarcasm or black humor. One worker used all the strategies.

> People give me a lot of grief. You know, you tell them where you work, and you tell them it's an animal shelter. And they say, "Well, you don't put them to sleep, do you?" And I always love to say, "Well, actually I give classes on how to do that," just for the shock value of it. Or it's the old, "I could never do what you do, I love animals too much." "Oh, I don't love them at all. That's why I work here. I kill them. I enjoy it." But sometimes you don't even mention where you work because you don't want to deal with it. It depends on the social situation I am in as to whether I want to go into it or not, and it also depends on how I feel at a given time. Some people are interested, and then I talk about spaying and neutering their pets.

Facing such external criticism, workers took comfort in belonging to the shelter community. Humor was one device that enhanced their feeling part of this special community, and it gave them a language for talking about death and their feelings. As with gallows humor in other settings, the argot was not particularly funny out of context; workers knew this, but learning to use it and find it humorous became a rite of passage. For instance, people telephoning the shelter might be greeted with the salutation "Heaven." Referring to the euthanasia room as "downtown" or the "lavender lounge" (the color of its walls) and the euthanasia drug as "sleepaway" or "go-go juice" (its brand name was "Fatal Plus") set the rather macabre tone.

But no ritual practice gave them a greater sense of we-ness than actually killing animals. No single act admitted them more firmly into the shelter community or more clearly marked the transition of shelter workers from the novice role. As they gained experience with euthanasia, workers developed a firmer sense of being in the same boat with peers who did what they did. They shared an unarticulated belief that others could not understand what it was like to kill unless they had also done so; even within the shelter, kennel workers often felt misunderstood by the front-desk people. As one worker reflected, "It does feel like you can't understand what I do if you can't understand that I don't like to kill, but that I have to kill. You'd have to see what I see. Maybe then." Since outsiders did not share this experience, workers tended to give them little credibility and to discount their opinions. By not communicating with others about it and thus curtailing the possibility of being understood, workers furthered their solidarity and created barriers between themselves and outsiders that shielded them from external criticism and diminished the uncomfortable feelings easily raised by the "uninformed" or "naive."

The Imperfection of Emotion Management

Certainly, shelter workers' capacity for killing animals was facilitated by acquiring an institutional self that provided them with a new set of on-the-job feelings. Yet it would be wrong to characterize these people, including those with many years' experience, as completely detached. Their strategies were far from perfect. It would be more accurate to say that their institutional socialization was incomplete. All the workers, including the very seasoned ones, felt uneasy about euthanasia at certain times.

For the few who continued to experience sharp and disturbing feelings, quitting was the most decisive way to manage emotions. One worker felt "plagued" by conflict; her own feelings for the animals made killing hard to accept, but intellectually she supported the shelter's euthanasia policy. She said it was "like having two people in my head, one good and the other evil, that argue about me destroying these animals." Feeling "guilty" about deaths she found "hard to justify," after nine months on the job, she quit.

For most workers this conflict was neither intense nor constant, but manifested itself as episodic uneasiness. From time to time, euthanasia provoked modest but clearly discernible levels of emotional distress. There was no consensus, however, on what kind of euthanasia would rattle people and make them feel uncomfortable, but everyone was unnerved by at least one form.

The most obvious discomfort with euthanasia occurred when workers had to kill animals to whom they were attached or whom they could easily see as pets. Although newcomers were more likely to have formed these attachments, seasoned workers could still be troubled by euthanasia when certain animals reminded them of other attachments. As one veteran worker reflected,

> I haven't been emotionally attached to a dog, except for one, for quite a while. I know my limit. But there are times when I'll look at a dog when I'm euthanizing it and go, "You've got Rex's eyes." Or it's an Irish setter—I have a natural attachment to Irish setters. Or black cats—I hate to euthanize black cats. It's real hard for me to euthanize a black cat.

Even without attachments, many workers found it "heartbreaking" to euthanize young, healthy, and well-behaved animals who could have become pets. Without a medical or psychological reason for it, euthanasia seemed a "waste."

For many workers, the procedure became unsettling if it appeared that animals were suffering physically or psychologically. This happened when injection of the euthanasia drug caused animals to "scream," "cry," or become very disoriented and move about frantically, but it also happened when animals seemed to "know" they were about to be killed or sensed that "death was in the air." "Cats aren't dumb. They know what's going on. Whenever you take them to the room, they always get this stance where their head goes up, and they know," observed one worker. Another said that many animals can "smell" death. These caretakers became uneasy because they assumed that the animals were "scared." "What is hard for me," said one yet another, "is when they are crying and they are very, very scared." Another shelter worker said that she could "feel their tension and anxiety" in the euthanasia room. "They seem to know what's happening—that something is going to happen," she added to explain her discomfort.

Ironically, for some workers, the opposite situation left them feeling unsettled. They found it eerie when animals were not scared and instead cooperated docilely. According to one worker, certain breeds were likely to act this way as they were being killed. She elaborated, "Greyhounds and Dobermans will either give you their paw or willingly give you their leg and look right past you. It's as though they are cooperating. The other dogs will look right at you."

Killing large numbers of animals in a single day was disconcerting for nearly everyone. This happened to one worker when the number of animals killed was so great she could not conceptualize the quantity until she picked up the thick pile of "yellow slips" (surrender forms), or saw by the drug log how many animals had been given euthanasia injections. The flow of animals into the shelter was seasonal, and workers grew to loathe those months when so many animals were brought in and euthanized. The summer was a particularly bad time for caretakers because so many cats came through. As one worker said, "They are constantly coming in. On a bad day, you might have to do it fifty times. There are straight months of killing." Another worker observed, "After three hours of killing, you come out a mess. It drains me completely. I'll turn around and see all these dead animals on the floor around me—and it's 'what have I done?'" And yet another worker noted:

> It's very difficult when we are inundated from spring until fall. Every single person who walks through the door has either a pillow case, a box, a laundry basket, or whatever—one more litter of kittens. And you only have x number of cages in your facility, and they are already full. So the animal may come in the front door and go out the back door in a barrel. It's very difficult if that animal never had a chance at life, or has had a very short life.

Even the veterans said that it "does not feel right" to spend so much time killing, particularly when so many of the animals were young and never had a chance to become a pet.

All workers, then, experienced at least some uneasiness when facing certain aspects of euthanasia, despite their socialization into the shelter's culture. The emotions generated by these situations overruled attempts by the shelter to help them manage their emotions and objectify their charges. When emotion management and objectification failed, workers felt some degree of connection and identification with the animals, which in turn elicited feelings of sadness, worry, and even remorse.

The initial conflict faced by shelter newcomers was extreme—because of their erst while perspective toward animals, killing them generated emotions that caused workers to balk at carrying out euthanasia. On closer inspection, however, this tension was replaced by a more moderate and digestible version of the same conflict. The conflict was repackaged and softened, but it was there, nonetheless. Shelter workers could more easily live with this version, and their emotion-management strategies got them to this point.

These strategies embodied an underlying dilemma between the simultaneous pulls toward objectifying the animals, on the one hand, and seeing the animals in pet-related terms, on the other—a conflict between rational necessity and sentiment, between head and heart, between the common perspective and that of a specialized institution, and between treating creatures in Martin Buber's (1958) I–It fashion—as deindividualized things quite different from oneself— or in an I–Thou manner—in which the other is acknowledged as kin.

A final look at these strategies reveals this underlying tension. By transforming shelter animals into virtual pets, the animals could be objectified, to some degree, while also categorizing them as something akin to yet different from, ordinary pets. When it came to actually killing them, workers could play the role of highly skilled technicians efficiently dispatching animal lives seen as not worth living, while simultaneously trying to take the emotional and physical feelings of animals into account. They viewed being able to avoid or postpone killing as a struggle between emotion and rationality; more significantly this much was allowed, thereby acknowledging some degree of emotion but within limits that reaffirmed a more rational approach. When it came to their view of pet owners (perhaps a collective projection of a sort), it was the public, and not themselves, that objectified animals; whatever they did, including the killing, paled by comparison, and it was done out of feeling and caring. Indeed, outsiders were regarded as a distant and alien group, while workers increasingly cultivated a strong sense of we-ness on the job—humans, too, seem to have two fundamentally different kinds of relations with one another.

It is not surprising that a tension persisted in the way that many shelter workers approached their animals, since the object–pet dichotomy is built into contemporary society and is behind many vagaries of human-animal interaction. Animals clearly play dual roles—utilitarian and affectional—in the lives of many people. For example, a person may regard some animals of the same species as pets and others as objects, as when a cockfighter retires a favorite, perhaps permanently injured rooster, to the sedentary life of a barnyard fowl, despite the fact that its fighting and stud days are over (Herzog 1989). Sometimes a person regards the same animal as both pet and object, as the southern, rural American hunter does who sees his dog as a significant partner for hunting and guarding, symbolically valued for its fidelity and rare abilities, but still treats it callously as a valueless item (Jordan 1975). And sometimes different people regard the same animal as either an object or a pet, as some children taking riding lessons—view a horse as little more than a cross-country vehicle, while others relate to it as a companion (Lawrence 1988).

It is also not surprising that these strategies were sometimes imperfect, failing to prevent the customary perspective toward animals from penetrating the shelter's. Even the most effective programs of organizational socialization are likely to be fallible when workers face situations that trigger their prior feelings and concerns. Many shelter workers may have felt uneasy because at certain times their personal, everyday thinking and feeling about animals in general may have taken precedence over the institutional "rules" for thinking and feeling about them. Moreover, such uneasiness is increasingly supported by the growing societal attention to the ideal of humaneness and concern for the moral status of animals (Rollin 1989).

Yet, in the end, by relying on these strategies workers reproduced the institution (e.g., Smith and Kleinman 1989), thereby creating a new generation of workers who would support the humane society model and the kind of human-animal relationship in which people could believe they were killing animals with a conscience. Far from being a unique situation, the shelter workers' relationship with animals is just our general culture's response to animals writ small. It is not likely that we ourselves are altogether exempt from this inconsistency, as our individual ways of managing our thoughts and feelings may similarly dull the conflict just enough for it to become a nagging uneasiness. For shelter workers, the conflict is merely heightened and their struggle to make peace with their acts, more deliberate and collective.

chapter 5

Systems of Meaning
in Primate Labs

> When I'm on the train . . . people would start looking at us. We'd be talking about our babies—Donna and Joan—and people would obviously think we were talking about children.
>
> —Technician at "Urban" Lab for Primate Research

> They're not people. I mean, they're not even like your dog at home. They're wild animals that sometimes need to be hit with a shovel or wrestled down.
>
> —Technican at "Ivy" Lab for Primate Research

ALL CULTURES PROVIDE their members with explanations for common occurrences in the human experience, accounting for distinctions between life and death, men and women, good and evil. According to some anthropologists, these explanations tend to be simple and uniform within premodern societies; there is little disagreement about them, because people rarely communicate with members of other societies, and their experiences have been largely the same. To be a member of these relatively homogenous and stable societies is to take for granted that there is only one meaning to reality. Of such societies, Jack Douglas (1971, 17) writes that it is "obvious that any man of 'good will' with 'adequate senses' will 'see' the meaning of things in just the way any such member of that society sees them." When a unified world view exists, distinctions between humans and animals will be clear and agreed upon by virtually everyone. For instance, the traditional

Balinese define animals as creatures that are hairy, walk on four legs, and have sharp teeth; humans are defined as the opposite. Thus, the Balinese maintain this distinction by not allowing babies to crawl, filing their teeth flat at puberty, and regarding hairy persons as demons (Nash and Sutherland 1991).

Contemporary industrial societies, on the other hand, generally are composed of people from a variety of cultures. They do not have a single system of meaning to explain fundamental distinctions. Instead, many voices interpret experience. In these complex, variegated, open, changing, and internally conflictive societies, multiple voices emanate, according to Burkart Holzner (1968), from different communities—religious, ideological, or occupational. Each community, he argues, is unified by a common epistemology and frame of reference that enables its members to agree on "the" proper perspective for the construction of reality. Thus, while definitions of reality are rarely shared on a societywide basis, members of each epistemic community truly share their versions of reality.

On closer inspection, however, there may not be a single, shared perspective within any epistemic community. Although the community may try to put a protective membrane around its knowledge, it is not impervious to the wide diversity of meanings in the larger society that its members can draw upon and express. More than likely, the small groups and individual organizations that compose an epistemic community will produce their own "local" meanings, different from the proper meaning that the community assumes. Of course, an epistemic community may claim that it has a unified and shared viewpoint, but such claims may be more mythic than real.

By Holzner's definition, biomedical science would certainly be considered an epistemic community. If so, it may also proclaim a mythic perspective for its workers. Those who conduct experiments on animals are assumed to regard and treat lab animals neither as pets that might be loved nor as objects that might be mistreated, but as instruments that have no meaning beyond their scientific one. However, a variety of perspectives toward animals exist in society (Kellert 1978, 1980), and workers can draw upon any of these constructs to define and guide their actual, everyday encounters with lab animals. These constructions of animals in laboratories sometimes can be at odds with each other in the scientific community just as they can be in everyday life. Arluke carried out in-depth field studies of two biomedical laboratories in order to examine whether the mythic animal of science existed in labs or whether nonscientific definitions prevailed. He chose these labs for study because they conducted similar experiments on primates and were located in the same geographical region of the country. In the two settings, Arluke conducted more than one hundred hours of unrestricted observation and seventy-five formal interviews, particularly focusing on the work of animal caretakers and technicians. As we see below, these workers were known as "cowboys" at Ivy Primate Lab because they took a utilitarian view of their charges, and as "animal people" at Urban Primate Lab because they morally elevated their animals.

Meaning Systems in Primate Labs

The Utilitarian Animal

Prospective technicians typically sought work at Ivy to get salaried jobs with good benefits, such as free tuition and health coverage. Some were drawn to Ivy also because the work was physical and often performed outdoors. As one "cowboy" said, "I like being outside, and I don't mind getting sweaty. I'm not the kind that can do desk work. I'd go crazy." Few came to Ivy specifically to work with animals. As one worker put it, "It's just a job. We come in and get our paychecks and get the hell out of here. And that's it."

Cowboys did not think of primates as interesting or appealing animals; they saw them only as work. Because of this, they did not use their free time to play or socialize with primates. One person described this lack of engagement:

> Do you think it is fun? The first month you work here it's fun. It's like working in a pizza place. The first day it's great, you eat pizza

all day long. The second day, you're kind of sick of pizza. Just like here. I work with the animals all day long. Everyone has free time, but playing with the animals isn't all that great. I would rather go out with some friends and party than stay and play with an animal.

Not only did relationships among people take precedence over spending extra time with animals, but the commitment of cowboys to the animals was weak enough on occasion to compromise basic veterinary care. Doing "just a job," they sometimes failed to complete their duties because they were "in a hurry to get the hell out of here." One caretaker, for instance, went home an hour early, leaving ten animals with empty water bottles, while another worker forgot to feed his monkeys before going home, leaving them "squealing for their food. You can tell when they're hungry. Nobody fed them. Somebody left."

Cowboys saw the primates as having unattractive personalities. As one described them, "I don't get attached because of their personality, their demeanor. They're kind of nasty little creatures, I think. Every single one, you walk into their room and they give you this scowl. It's their way of telling you, back off." Another cowboy noted, "Everyone likes monkeys in a zoo. I used to want a monkey as a pet. Wouldn't take one now. They're dirty, they smell, they're disgusting, they scratch, they bite." Several cowboys thought that an unnamed psychiatrist was very accurate when he said "that working with monkeys was like working with retarded children that have homicidal tendencies." One technician was grateful that he no longer worked with primates, preferring instead to work with mice.

I like mice because they don't make any noise. They don't bite and don't scratch. It's calming to me to work with them, to change their cages. You know, you pick them up and put them in another one. Whereas with monkeys, you're pulling out the pan, and they reach out and grab you and sometimes they pull your hair. Mice are just easier to work with. With monkeys, you have to push racks around and there's heavy lifting. You know, I have nothing against hard work at all, but, man, if I had a dollar for every time I pulled a muscle when I was working with monkeys. . . . I'd much rather clean a mouse cage and plop it back on the rack.

Living with Contradiction

Cowboys drew clear boundaries between humans and nonhuman primates and between domestic pets and their lab animals. One technician at Ivy who was preparing to quit because of the prevailing attitude, said, "The cowboys obviously think they are superior beings to these animals. It's the attitude—like how can you even say we're related to these animals. We're human beings. We're men. We're much better. And that is prevalent in the cowboy attitude." Speaking about his charges, one cowboy confessed,

> I think I am realistic. I like animals, but . . . let's be serious. They're not people. Some people here treat them like their pets. They're not your pets. You have a dog, and there are dogs used here. But these aren't your dogs here. Let's not be ridiculous. Same exact thing with the monkeys. You don't play with them all day long or stay here after work hours to do that.

From the cowboys' perspective, it was "ridiculous" to treat monkeys like humans, and those who did were considered misguided. This distinction came up often, even over the matter of giving "treats" to the primates. As one worker complained:

> Some of them are ridiculous here. They treat the animals like they are almost people. They pretend that. I like the animals. If I get scratched—no, I don't like them. You know, "You asshole, why did you do that?" The girls, they've got to play the peanut tricks: "Hey, I'll give you an extra treat." Things they don't need. Like the marmosets. When we feed the animals, we give them monkey chow and maybe a couple pieces of fruit here and there. If you come back from lunch and you have a candy bar, you'd give them a little piece—the ones you like. But an average feeding for the CJs [monkeys] where Amy is, she would do yogurt, crickets, flies, butterscotch pudding— I mean, it's a disaster—bananas, apples, and they don't even eat most of it. It sits there. They have the vets convinced that they like this food. They're not going to get any of that stuff in the wild. And they did fine in the wild. You don't get half the stuff they get. Maybe fruit. They don't get monkey chow in the wild either, but monkey chow is made just for monkeys. It looks like dog food. You probably couldn't tell the difference. It's like a regular dog biscuit.

Cowboys did not cultivate fond or nurturing attachments with their charges and instead depersonalized primates, treating them as if they were "a piece of furniture." For example, a few of the technicians named the animals, but cowboys rarely used these names or used them incorrectly. A cowboy elaborated, "If I need an animal in B1, I will ask for number 226-85. A lot of them are named stupid names—whatever they look like, or a friend of yours. There's one over there now called Zorba but some people call him Baby Doll and somebody else calls him something stupid." Nor did cowboys "talk to the monkeys. I never even play with them." Not surprisingly, cowboys were unfazed by the death of primates. As one technician related, "We had someone who pushed a monkey by accident into the cage washer. It died. The water is extremely hot. It burned to death. If it happened to me, the only thing I would feel badly about would be someone getting mad at me cause I did it. I certainly wouldn't cry about it."

Cowboys sometimes teased or were rough with primates so they could maintain their "authority" over them, amuse themselves, or discharge anger. One worker observed, "People here think they have to abuse them and tease them to exert their authority over them. They think they have to just go in and smack the cages with bars and knock the shit out of the animals to show them who's boss." For example, most technicians ignored and looked away from primates if they made open-mouth threats to them, but some cowboys returned the threat by making heckling sounds or banging on the cage bars. If a monkey grabbed or scratched a cowboy as he walked by the cage, he might "retaliate." As one cowboy explained:

> If I walk by a cage and get scratched or bitten, you do things just like a police officer would do by "accident"—you know, you catch me doing something wrong and you bump into me on purpose and say, "Oops, sorry about that." The temptation is there to just pull the squeeze bar right out to just hit them up against the cage. A lot of people do that, but won't admit it. You just get mad. They're not going to remember, they'll do it again, but basically you're satisfied.

In rare instances, workers might strike an animal. Arluke was shown one monkey with a permanently dislocated jaw. He was told that the animal was either "hit by a shovel or punched by an animal careworker terrorizing it." Sometimes the teasing was random "amusement." One worker, for instance, thought it was funny to throw rocks at some of the animals, and another worker gave them Coke cans knowing that they could cut themselves on the sharp metal edges.

Cowboys were most concerned about getting their work done as fast as possible and resorted to methods that they thought were expedient. When monkeys were removed from their cages, cowboys would "knock down" (anesthetize) the animals because it was quicker and easier for them, while a few others, who were teased for it, tried to train the animals to leave their cages on a collar. In order to inject the monkeys with tranquilizers, cowboys were likely to scare rather than talk the animals into position, and they enjoyed doing this. As one cowboy noted, "I like scaring them—you know, scaring them up to the front so you can knock them down. You go in there with a shovel—like 'Come on! gaa! haa!' They don't like shovels because they've been hit with shovels. It's more of a scare thing—you go—'get back! get back!' And they come at you a little bit and you kind of poke them." If scaring failed, they might hit the animals with shovels to get them into transfer cages.

When groups of monkeys had to be caught without the use of tranquilizers, cowboys called it a "rodeo." In the words of one technician, "If you throw out chemical restraint, then you have to be physical—that's the cowboy—you have to go in there and wrestle them and you get worn down. They want to get loose. It's just a very, very physical way to go about it. There's finesse involved in it—like the finesse in a prizefighter." One worker recounted how he learned to catch monkeys:

> What happened to me was that they gave me a pair of gloves and showed me a cage that was about half the size of this office. There was one big monkey in it, and they said, "Go get it" and stood outside in the hallway and laughed. They thought it was the funniest

thing in the world. And I got him! I'd be damned if I was going to go out and face these guys without this monkey. I had to wrestle him.

Another cowboy pointed out the risks involved in "wrestling" primates:

> You basically have to wrestle with them. They are in such a high level of emotion, it's not unusual if you grab an animal by its arm the wrong way, they'll try to get away from you and break their own arm. I've seen this happen. So you're in a situation where you don't want to get hurt, but you don't want to hurt the animal. But there's going to be a winner and a loser here.

During these "roundups," workers would frenetically catch large numbers of monkeys by scaring them and pinning them to cage bars with nets and injecting them with tranquilizers. As the drug took effect, some were caught in nets held by workers while others would drop haphazardly to the cage floor. One technician critical of cowboys described these sessions:

> The animals basically fall down after they are injected. If they see them dropping down, they'll try to catch them with nets, but sometimes they are busy and boom! They'll just fall down. It seems incredibly chaotic and stressful to the animals. It's done so fast, they treat them like meat. It reminds me of factory work where you hurry up and build something really fast.

Cowboys particularly welcomed monkey escapes, seeing these chaotic moments as diversions from otherwise boring work and as a chance to match their strength against the animals' in what they defined as "dangerous" encounters. "It's a change in the day," one cowboy remarked about the opportunity to "wrestle" primates on the loose. Some cowboys saw the capturing as fun and exciting, comparing it to a hockey game when it took place in the hallways or to tracking and hunting when animals got out into the neighboring woods. "I like the chase when an animal gets loose," a cowboy said enthusiastically. He also noted:

> If you can't knock it down by pinning it and hitting it with the syringe, it's exciting because you have to catch them. It's like . . . kind

Living with Contradiction

of dangerous. I mean, it's you against the animal. He's running around. You have to actually catch him by hand. Somehow you have to pin the head down right away so he can't bite you, and put his arms behind his back. It's real scary the first couple of times. . . . Yeah, the chase is fun.

Given the cowboys' perspective toward their animal work, it was not surprising that they did little to improve the well-being of primates. Although they saw their monkeys as being in "jail," and acknowledged that the animals were likely to be "unhappy," cowboys felt that their charges' state was unalterable. As one put it, "They are not happy anyway. They're in cages. You can't really make them happy." Cowboys resented suggestions about exercising animals or creating stimulating situations for them because this meant more work, and they doubted the value of these efforts. Some pointed to the fact that, although the animals were confined and used for experiments, they never had to worry about finding food or being killed by wild animals, "So they don't have it so bad. It's like being in jail. You get fed. You get fed in jail, you get fed here. That's about it."

Morally Elevated Animals

Many technicians had sought work at Urban Primate Lab because they wanted a job with animals. According to one technician, "A few are here because they need the money and they need a job, but most are here because of the animals. I feel like everybody here is an animal person." Many saw working with primates in particular as an "unbelievable opportunity," although most had reservations about using primates for research. One worker spoke of her ambivalence, "None of us are here because we think it's great that these animals are undergoing laboratory experimentation. We're not here because we think AIDS research is so important that we have to take care of these animals so they can participate. I don't think you'll find one person here who thinks along those lines." A number of workers frankly stated that they "wished these animals were not in research. I really wish they were not, but they are. And I'm not living in la-la land. I'm living with the reality that the animals are here. If I thought that by my leaving today these animals would not be in research, I would go. But if I leave and go onto something that has less stress, these animals will still be here." Workers commonly were uncomfortable about using primates for research because they were so closely related to humans. As one caretaker noted, "You have to think—if they are so close to us, why are we doing this to them? I mean why are we doing this if they understand what we are saying?"

Their interest in and concern for the primates meant that workers often spent some of their free time during or after work with the animals, socializing with them because they enjoyed the interaction and also because they felt some animals "needed" it. One technician remarked, "If you have an extra ten minutes, you are going to spend it with someone you really care about or someone that really needs you." Visiting the nursery, for example, was a popular activity for many technicians, both male and female. During their breaks, they frequently stopped by to play with young primates and, in so doing, they sometimes developed special relationships with them that they felt enriched their jobs. Speculating on the motivation for these visits, one animal person said, "We have people who work with the adult chimps that come over and play with animals during their lunch hour. Now is it because they are being altruistic and they're saying, 'I'm going to spend my half-an-hour really doing something for these animals' or is it, 'Hey, I'm going to go in there and they're going to climb all over me and they are going to hug me and kiss me and they like me.'" Another worker simply said, "I get an enormous amount of gratification from the animals." Some of Urban's workers even talked about the problem of learning to stop themselves from paying too much attention to the animals because their work would never get done if they indulged their curiosity and affection.

Urban's animal people were more likely to see their charges as having individual and appealing personalities than the cowboys who attributed a corporate and negative personality to them. And their descriptions of individual animals were more nuanced than those given by cowboys. Animal people had respect, even awe, for many of their charges: "I was so amazed when they first showed me the adults—'look at them!'—I mean, they're just so big and real. You know, when you look into a chimpanzee's eyes you have the feeling of a totally sentient being—a real creature, a real intelligence there looking back at you. You know there's something there." One typical worker at Urban, for instance, spoke with interest and sensitivity about the personalities of two of her animals, freely anthropomorphizing and psychologizing their behaviors—practices cowboys rarely engaged in:

> Some of them seem to have a sense of outrage. Like Danny is very demanding and he'll get very angry if you don't pay attention to him, but then an animal like Alan, no matter how many times you are nasty to him, I mean we are never really nasty to them, he never gets angry. But Danny gets angry if you walk away and pay attention to anyone except him. I think when he was young, he got a lot of attention, so consequently he isn't very mature yet. He gets very jealous.

They frequently established strong, nurturing bonds with "favorites" and formed unobjectified relationships with many others. People spoke somewhat possessively about particular animals being "theirs," and fellow workers were generally aware of these special attachments. "Most people have theirs. I have to say, it's almost like an ownership. For some it might be a mother or father type thing. For others, it's still an animal, but it's very special. It's very special. Mary has Benjamin—that's her baby." Many workers who formed powerful attachments were often distressed and saddened because of them. Talking about one of her peers, a worker said:

> Doug continues to take chances with his animals as I do with my animals. He is very, very attached to his animals and feels grief when something happens to them. He suffers, he really suffers. He really does. He gets angry, depressed. He's probably too close to the animals. He can't draw that line. I think a lot of us fear going over the edge where you become too involved.

Not surprisingly, then, practices such as naming animals were important to animal people, and they often used the names when interacting with animals or referring to them with fellow workers. The same animal names would be honored and used by different workers as well as by most scientists and veterinarians at Urban.

Their relationship with animals was based on negotiation rather than on control and power, as it was for cowboys. According to one worker at Urban, it was important to learn to "bargain" with primates rather than try and overpower them: "You share control of the situation and have to bargain with them. Just because you are on the outside of the cage, you do not have control." Workers talked less about establishing control over primates and more about "respecting" their strength, as one admitted: "I respect the fact that they can hurt me. You don't expect that a human child is going to bite you or hit you or knock your head against the wall. Whereas these animals will hurt me, although they may not do it viciously."

Compared to Ivy, where cowboys' interactions with animals were instrumental and measured by how much time it took to complete tasks, interactions at Urban tended to be affective, premised on establishing communication with animals and a certain degree of reciprocity, if not egalitarianism, in their relationships. One worker noted, "They'll come right up to the cage and look at you and they expect you to have that eye-to-eye contact, and sometimes they want mouth-to-mouth contact." Animal lovers not only talked to their animals, but assumed that they understood much of what was said. As one technician speculated, "I think they do understand. I really think they understand a lot. It's not like a dog that responds to your tone. These animals understand words. I even make it a habit not to talk about them in front of them in case they understand." Another worker provided in more detail:

We all have our little stories that we can tell about the fact that we are sure they understand what we are talking about because they will come in on cue. Mine is two weeks ago. I was leaving for Florida, and it was important to me that Jonah and Emma say good-bye to me in some kind of way. I needed it. I just thought I had to explain to them that I was going away, that I hoped they'd be good. That they wouldn't give anybody any trouble. Make sure they knew that I was coming back. I said to them, "Just before I go, one time, would you sign 'friend' for me?" Friend is with the two index fingers up. Usually I just put one index finger up to the cage and sometimes they will do it, but not usually on cue. It's usually a mistake. And this particular time I said, "Jonah, would you sign 'friend' for me just this one time?" And I put my finger up and he put his finger out . . . and he did it just as clear as it could be. And I said, "Emma, what about you? Will you sign 'friend' for me?" And she did it also. I really got the feeling that they understood that this was important to me. Usually they won't do it on cue. We all have stories where we're sure that they understand. And we can't prove it. It's not scientific, but I think we also need to believe that they understand we care about them.

Many felt that they got back "something" from the primates. As a worker said, "That animal gives me something. As much as I give to it, it has given back to me." For some workers, this was "love and affection." One technician, for instance, talked about how some of the primates "adopted" her and sought to protect her: "My animals have adopted me as one of theirs, and if anybody tries to hurt me, they will attack them. I saw it when we had a camera crew here last year. One of the TV technicians was fitting me for a microphone and wanted to clip it to my uniform on the collar, and as he did this, Billy attacked him. I guess he thought this man was hurting me." Some talked about "trusting" their animals' reactions to new people as a way of appraising their character. One of them asserted, "I trust Lisa and Seth's judgment." When Lisa or Seth "could not deal" with strangers, it was a warning flag for her to exercise caution. "I would say, I don't know about this guy. I would say, let's go easy."

Most found it difficult to draw distinct boundaries between humans and their charges. Those who worked in the nursery found this almost impossible. One caretaker, for instance, thought of herself as a surrogate mother to babies whose needs were indistinguishable from those of human infants. Her attachment to them, she thought, was equivalent to the connection she imagined having with human infants: "I never had so many maternal urges as I do with these guys.

I was telling my mom I was going to go through postpartum depression when I leave here. When I'm away on the weekend, by Monday I miss them so much I'm happy to come back. I never dread Mondays. I'm always looking forward to them because I miss them." Another nursery caretaker reported:

> Very often when I am on the train with Laura, we would start talking about things and people would start looking at us. We'd be talking about our babies—Donna and Joan—and people would obviously think we were talking about children. And we'd talk about changing diapers, changing formulas, and feeding bottles, and then we'd say, "Who should we cage Joan with, shall we put her with Linda?" and people would look at us and be so startled.

Those who worked with adult animals came to view their favorites through categories such as "friends" or "buddies" that did not clearly separate animals from humans. A worker observed, "It's hard. The boundaries are very fuzzy. People have to create new boundaries because it's not so much human and primate as human and this animal which is very close. I mean—if you want to get religious—if there is a heaven, is there a chimp heaven? Who knows."

As the boundaries blurred, some animal people saw their own behavior changing in noticeable ways. Several mentioned that since coming to Urban they found themselves acting like primates or putting themselves literally into the situations faced by their charges. One worker, for instance, said that he spent several hours inside an empty cage because he wanted to know what it was like. Workers talked openly with fellow workers, albeit jokingly, about lapses into animal behaviors. A worker said of herself and a friend, "One day we caught each other doing very primate things. She said, 'You don't know I have such a hard time' [not acting this way]. I find that when I'm around other people here, we very often do very primate things. And it's understood and it's appreciated." Another worker noted:

> I mean, I'll go to the supermarket, and if I see a nice cantaloupe, the first thing I want to do is go "hah-hah-hah-hah" [primate food

Living with Contradiction

bark] and sometimes I forget myself. . . . Their vocalization is very concise and clear . . . . Very often if I get excited I want to go like this [makes facial expression with mouth] because that says it more than my saying to you, "Well, I'm very happy that we are sitting here talking." If I were to go like this, you would know.

Even those who did not see their animals in human terms, still regarded them very highly. For instance, one worker said, "I talk to them, and I'll say, 'Let's be friends. You're a good friend.' But I think that's more talking than meaning. I don't think of them as . . . it's not really like a mother, although you love them all and you take care of them all, and you would never abuse any, you would never ignore any."

The psychological well-being of their charges had a high priority for many workers at Urban. The fact that they had "fuzzy" boundaries between themselves and their animals made it likely that they would perceive the animals as unhappy. One worker, for instance, talked about how primates "do very human things—they do laugh and they do smile. They show very human characteristics. I know when there's something wrong with them even if they don't bang their heads against the cage or chew their fingers." Many of their steps to provide increased stimulation for animals only further confounded the boundaries between species. One caretaker, for example, told how distressed she was because the animals were caged: "Just the fact that they are in cages bothers me a lot. These creatures are amazing, and it's almost like a racism on our part to decide that they don't have the right to do what they want to do. I try to push that issue aside because I know if I think about it, I'm not going to make it." Workers were very concerned about their animals being bored, but felt that human interaction and not just mechanical devices were required to provide adequate stimulation. As one worker noted, "I feel like a lot of our animals are psychologically well adapted because they do get our attention. You can't just throw a paper bag in there and say 'play.' I mean, they will play, but they need human interaction." Of particular concern to the director and his workers was creating "a good childhood" for their primates, so that "hopefully, with that background, they will have what it takes to adapt to the adverse conditions they face."

Many technicians at Urban developed a missionary and addictive attitude toward their work with animals, as did shelter workers with their charges. "I try to do everything I can for them," commented one worker. Another said, "My job, my mission in life, is to see that they have a good life." Almost all of the workers emphasized that they felt a strong personal "responsibility" for their animals and thought that their efforts were "worthwhile" if they improved the lives of their primates. As one worker commented, "I feel that my days are very worthwhile—I've given something to all these animals. I worked with that group today and each one had enrichment. I talked with each one. I hugged them and scratched them or do whatever I can with them." Part of this addictive attitude stemmed from the belief held by some technicians that they were irreplaceable in their jobs because certain animals needed them. As one worker said of herself, "I'm exhausted when I go home and I wonder if I can get to work tomorrow, but the next day comes and I feel that I've got to be there. I know that somebody else will do my work if I am not here, but nobody will do it quite like I do. No one will take Jack and Flora out to play because they are too big and too wild to be handled by most anyone."

Managing for Meaning

The existence at Urban and Ivy labs of two such discrepant systems of meaning is in part the result of workers drawing from alternative societal meanings of animals and in part the way these meanings are interpreted and reinforced by key individuals having authority in each lab. Their authority is necessary to carry out what Holzner (1968) calls the "delicate process" of establishing a shared frame of reference—a process that requires the careful selection and shaping of people to share congruent values and the judicious exercise of power to structure interaction in ways that maintain the desired perspective.

Living with Contradiction

Research in corporate settings supports Holzner's thinking. Managers, for example, actively try to influence their workers' attitudes toward clients in order to create a single organizational point of view. Regardless of the thoroughness of the hiring process, managers still work to bring employees' thinking in line with the company's view of clients. One study (Bird et al. 1989) found that managers spoke a moral discourse that communicated particular norms to workers, while other research (Harris 1990) reported that workers frequently felt pressured to modify their values in order to achieve company goals set by managers. To understand, then, why different meaning systems existed at Ivy and Urban, it is necessary to look at the managerial style of key individuals who were empowered to select workers, serve as ethical models, and influence the character of supervision and social control.

Cowboy Control

At Ivy, the director of animal care—himself a technician—did the hiring of caretakers. When interviewing potential employees, he deliberately downplayed "the animal part"—discussion having to do with concerns about animals. In his words, "When I introduce the animal part, I tell them that we owe the animal the best veterinary care he can get, the best food, the best water, and the cleanliest environment we can give him. You owe that to anybody if you forced them to be some place. And that's our job." In assessing people, his biggest concern was to weed out "animal freaks," people who would be unwilling to clean up "monkey crap," and covert animal activists. Although his ideal candidate was someone raised on a farm who liked dirty and physical work, he was hesitant to hire someone who "comes in and starts talking to me about how proresearch they are, how they think we are doing great work out here, or people who want to come in and volunteer their time because they love animals and want to participate in research. I tend to shy away a little bit because I have some colleagues in the business that have been infiltrated by people from animal rights groups." He was comfortable hiring people who saw their work as just a job and had no special interest in animals or science. He noted, "Most of the people will be good workers. Forget research. Forget that esoterica. I mean, it's a paycheck. With these people it gets down to a very basic level—I offer you the job and you take it. We have an agreement—you do the work, I give you money. That's it, and that's fine."

At Ivy, those people with formal authority set a moral tone by defining the institution as highly committed to the business of research. Workers' first priority was to research, and animals were merely a vehicle to that end. As one worker acknowledged, "This attitude comes down from management." No senior staff members made any effort consciously to model their behavior for the caretakers' benefit. The only role models were at a much lower level of authority—the head of animal care, for example—who supported cowboyism. Administrators sent clear messages to workers about institutional priorities that were understood by workers; for example, that clean floors were more important than dying monkeys.

> It's related from Adam—the assistant director here—on down.
> He's an army man. And to Adam, clean floors are important, clean
> walls are important, shiny this or shiny that is important. A lot of
> people are just trying to suck up to their superior. And that's what's
> being emphasized all the way down—you know, "This floor looks
> terrible." It doesn't matter that there's ten monkeys dead in the
> cage, but as long as the floors look shiny. They spent hundreds of
> thousands of dollars redoing floors here, but we have broken cages,
> bad equipment, we have untrained people here, but that's not a pri-
> ority. The floors are a priority. They feel that the animals are an
> overhead cost—their food, animal care—that's all in our base
> grant, and they want to cut that cost as much as possible. The ani-
> mals are mere equipment.

In the eyes of the few noncowboys, Ivy's laxness about primate care was further evidence of the low priority animal care had at their facility. Worse than indifferent care, as some workers claimed, were "cover-ups" of "negligence" that caused animal deaths. One worker lamented:

I find it so hard to get up in the morning. I don't want to come in because I know I'll see more of the same stuff, more of the same attitudes, what tragedy is going to happen next—and it's not only sickness. I mean there have been things that have happened here because of human negligence. Tragic, tragic things, and nobody was held accountable or responsible for these things. Things that have caused death to the animals. There have been innumerable cases like this, I can't count them all.

In one such instance, it was alleged that four monkeys died from dehydration because poorly trained weekend staff did not check their water sippers, which had become clogged. As one worker exclaimed, "People were just dragging in monkeys like you wouldn't believe." No one was reprimanded and nothing was done to improve the training of weekend staff; the official explanation was that the animals died from tannic acid poisoning from eating acorns. A frustrated worker elaborated on the aftermath:

> There is cover-up of mismanagement here. Everybody knew there was a sipper clogged, but they decided that instead of being angry at management—that people aren't trained right—that somebody didn't see this—they just decided it must be poisoning. It really frustrated me because I was here and I saw all the animals die. I saw how they all looked when they came. I was told that many years ago that if something like that happened, somebody would either have been fired or there would have been a letter written in their file. But you don't see that happening any more.

In the absence of strong and clear managerial norms for interacting with animals, Ivy's cowboys became the de facto norm-setters, and did so primarily through the exercise of teasing and ridicule. Fellow workers might be teased if they were not "macho." One worker, for instance, was seen by cowboys as too careful and scared. He admitted, "Some other people are less intimidated than I am. Like this one guy—he used to call me a sissy because I used to be real timid in the cage, but I used to say, 'Hey, I'm just being careful.'" Those who chose less aggressive approaches to getting animals out of their cages were belittled by cowboys, as one cowboy tells us himself:

Some of the people here are ridiculous. If an animal gets out, I go in, catch it no matter how long it took by hand. I wouldn't play games. If one gets out on Bonnie, first we try to talk to it, say, "Come on, honey." Then we do the marshmallows. Then we throw some food into the cage. Then we'd try and just scare it with a squeegee—not touch it. It's stupid. And then we try a pole syringe without a syringe on it, so it's like using a pool cue. It's a whole, big disaster.

People also might be teased if they wore protective clothing such as gloves and masks around monkeys; cowboys saw this policy as a "hassle" or "pain in the neck" and usually disregarded it. Efforts by a few to improve the well-being of primates or even provide basic medical care also met with ridicule. To cowboys, these efforts "were foolish and just made more work." One new worker, for instance, objected to cowboys putting their fingers on needles before inserting them into medication bottles because of contamination. She said, "They gave me a hard time and called me 'good-housekeeping woman' or 'Miss Tidybowl' because I was concerned about that stuff." In another incident, a worker moved a monkey away from two big rhesus males that upset him so much that he had seizures. However, cowboys moved him back next to the big males, criticized the worker for being too sensitive, and wrote a letter to her supervisor saying that she was "having emotional outbursts." One worker said of the cowboys, "They will cut you down at every point they can. They will hinder you every time you try to do things for the animals."

Cowboys also built reputations by taking risks in handling animals, especially the big and strong ones. One worker noted, "When monkeys have to be caught in their cages, people are, like, 'He can go out and catch a monkey for me but nobody else can do it because it is so dangerous.' Their attitude is that only they can catch animals and this is how they obtain status." One cowboy, for instance, was lauded for his daring: "He was unbelievable. You know, the monkey's going over his head, and he'll just reach up and grab it with his hand without catching gloves. And he's never been bit. When he

Living with Contradiction

goes into the cage to clean it out, usually you block the animals on one side and clean the other side, but he doesn't even block." Cowboys were proud to work with what they called "real monkeys" and made fun of those who worked with "not real monkeys," the former being large, strong adult animals that could be risky to handle, while the latter were small or young animals that offered little risk. A marmoset worker confirmed this:

> Most people here say they look like rodents and make jokes that they aren't real monkeys. We are put down because we don't work with the real monkeys. It's a size thing—they're small. They're not the big rhesus and baboons. It's the same thing with the nursery, even though they may have rhesus monkeys in there, they are the babies. If you work in the nursery, you're the butt of a lot of jokes.

The Rule of Animal People

At Urban, the veterinarian assumed the major responsibility for the hiring of technicians. "I let the animals do the hiring," he proudly remarked. Prospective employees were always observed around the animals to see how they reacted to the primates and how the primates reacted to them. Through these trial meetings, he hoped to find job candidates with a genuine interest in and a desire to communicate with the primates. He particularly looked for applicants who were ambivalent about using animals for medical research, believing that people uncritical of it would not be as good around the animals. His predominant concern was to hire people highly committed to the primates' general well-being, including but not limited to basic feeding and cleaning.

Workers at Urban were aware that the veterinarian modeled his behavior for them and, for the most part, respected that model and tried to emulate it. As one technician commented, "He is a model for me personally and for most of the people who work here. He is always aware that people are watching him. We know his thoughts are uppermost for the animals." Another worker praised the director:

His attitudes are like those of someone who came out of vet school last year. His philosophy is that animals deserve to have the very best possible conditions. He is an advocate for the animals here. He always puts them foremost. I hope I can meet that challenge as well. He is a good mentor for me in that respect because he sometimes pushes me—you know, "Gee, I should be reaching out that way, too."

Workers saw the director as both "preaching and practicing" a policy of devotion to the well-being of lab animals, and one worker elaborated on his own commitment: "They're here, but they didn't ask to be here. They don't have a choice, so I think it is incumbent upon us to make their lives as meaningful and as rich as possible under the circumstances. And this is what Dr. Smith preaches, and he practices what he preaches." He was very demonstrative with the animals, giving them emotionally lavish greetings by hugging and kissing infants, and his affection for the animals was apparent to workers even in the way he spoke to them. A worker commented on this, "He always talks with the animals, and that allows the rest of us to be free to do so. And he loves and appreciates that we do it. He talks to them like they understand. He never discussed it, but I think he also thinks as I do, that if they don't understand, you haven't lost anything. But if they do understand, there are wonderful ramifications." He also did not appear to workers as uncompromisingly supportive of animal research. Another worker, in fact, reported this exchange:

I came from a point of view of being very big on animal rights. I told Dr. Smith that I needed to talk to someone who was not an animal rights person, but I needed the other viewpoint. And he said, which I think tells a lot about him, he said, "I'm not the other viewpoint. I'm not the lab viewpoint." This said a lot to me about him. He takes so much of his time to make people understand that all people who work in labs are not "scientists"—that scientists are not always against animal rights and that many of your lab people are pro–animal rights.

Thus, the director was seen as viewing and treating lab animals, according to one worker, as "living creatures that are not inanimate objects but feeling individuals."

Living with Contradiction

He sought openly to encourage and reward workers who made special efforts to care for the animals. One day while performing surgery on a primate, he peeked into an adjoining room where he saw one of the new caretakers talking to some primates. Beaming, he told the technicians working with him how pleased he was to see the new person talking with the animals, instead of being too embarrassed to do so, as some caretakers were. He also tried to create an environment where workers were comfortable about reporting inappropriate animal handling to him. One effort in this direction was the installation of a locked suggestion box in which workers could put anonymous allegations about coworkers' behavior.

At Urban, the director made it clear that abuse in any form was not tolerated, and workers were well aware of this position, as one confirmed, "He is quite intolerant of any kind of abuse, any kind of insensitivity to the animals. He never yells or screams. But he will give you a look that you know you've been chastised." Both the director and the other veterinarian identified themselves to workers more as advocates for animals than advocates for researchers, as opposed to Ivy's veterinarians who blurred advocacy and researcher roles. Another caretaker said of Urban's director:

> He reminds us to take into consideration how what you are doing to animals will affect them, or how can you make it so that there is the least abuse; I shouldn't say "abuse," least pain or least damage. And that could be how to get an animal out of the cage or not anesthetizing an animal more than once a week. He always tries to remind us to take little things like that into consideration—it's the little things that add up to your attitude toward research animals.

Status among animal people, as for the cowboys, was determined by how they worked with their charges. At Urban, however, reputations hinged on how well animals seemed to respond to technicians: "There is almost a competitiveness about being with the animals. Your general ability to get along with animals is very important here for how you are seen. If the animals don't like you, that's bad news, even though no one says it like that; I think there is a tacit understanding about that." This emphasis on animals, as one worker put it, "sometimes engenders frustration because the technicians feel the animals come first and the technicians are not important. I hear the grumbling, but that's usually from the people who are really not all that interested in the animals. Maybe they're here for some other reason." In part, reputations also stemmed from unusual demonstrations of commitment to animals in need. A few workers, including the chief veterinarian, had taken infant primates home to nurse because they had been rejected by their mothers. These efforts were informally praised and respected.

Quite disparate systems of meaning regarding animals can exist in modern societies, even when the same type of setting is examined. Of course, such systems of meaning are not always completely separable, and this was evidenced by the small pockets of resistance to the dominant meanings that existed at both Ivy and Urban laboratories. A few technicians at Ivy shared the views held by Urban's animal people, while the reverse was true at Urban. Moreover, not all the scientists bought into the prevailing meanings of animals at Ivy and Urban. Occasionally, clashes did occur at both facilities over the meaning of primates in science and the behavior that was appropriate toward them, although the disputes were invariably resolved in favor of the predominant system of meaning in each setting.

Yet on the whole, both settings had remarkably homogenous systems of meaning—but the mythic animal of science existed in neither. Apparently, the "real," working definition of animals will be determined by the local culture of individual laboratories and facilities rather than by the ideology of science. Actual rather than ideal norms will arise in specific situations that guide the behavior of individuals in their interactions with animals, and the dynamics of their creation and enforcement will be no different from that of other norms—whether one is looking at how hard people work or how much gossip is tolerated. In Ivy's and Urban's systems of meaning at least, the mythic lab animal of science was nowhere in sight.

What is significant is not merely that alternative systems of meaning exist in laboratories, but that they do so without calling attention to this fact. For the most part, they seem to coexist effortlessly—even though they may be different from the mythic definition and inconsistent with each other—under the same cultural roof. This, too, may reflect modern society and the nature of its epistemic worlds. Although spokespeople who represent biomedical science would probably disapprove of alternative meanings of lab animals other than the mythic, official animal of science, they are too far removed from the everyday practice of science to be aware of these local meanings or to do anything to bring them more in line with the official definition. Local-level organizations are widely scattered throughout the country, and, except for word-of-mouth reports, neither spokespeople nor workers in other settings will know how their counterparts define lab animals elsewhere.

Moreover, if individuals discover meanings of animals that trouble them, there are usually norms that discourage intervention on other people's professional turf. And even if powerful individuals in the scientific community attempted to impose the image of the mythic lab animal, such attempts would be likely to fail because of the resilience of local systems of meaning. Quite clearly, the real—as opposed to the mythic—animal is a construction from the ground up, so to speak. To understand how these animals are defined and treated, one should bypass those who speak on behalf of the biomedical community and study those with the local power to influence the thinking and feeling of ordinary people who earn a living or pursue a career in the company of animals.

Finally, that the cowboys and the animal people could create such different systems of meaning speaks to the workers' ability to create or dissolve boundaries between themselves and the animals they worked with. It would be wrong, however, to think that such boundary work occurs only at the small-group level. It is a larger social process that is anchored in history and culture, and its operation is more complex than we have seen thus far. As we can observe in the next chapter, entire societies are imbued with boundary work.

chapter 6

Boundary Work in Nazi Germany

> In order that animal torturing shall not continue . . . I will commit
> to concentration camps those who still think that they can continue
> to treat animals as inanimate property.
>
> — Hermann Göring, radio broadcast, 1933

IT IS WELL KNOWN that the Nazis treated human beings with extreme cruelty. Grisly "medical" experiments on humans have been
carefully documented and analyzed (e.g., Lifton 1986), as has the
cold, calculated extermination of millions of people in the Holocaust (e.g., Hilberg 1961). Less well known are the extensive measures taken by the Nazis to ensure humane care and protection of
animals. Of course, other societies have also exhibited a disdain for
humans while also showing marked concern for animals, but the
extent to which humans were brutalized and animals were idolized
in Nazi Germany makes the others pale by comparison. In short,
Nazi Germany presents a striking case of inconsistency between the
species.

How could the Nazis have been so concerned about cruelty to animals while they treated people so inhumanely? Although it would

be easy to dismiss the apparently benevolent Nazi attitude toward animals as hypocrisy, this would be a facile way of ignoring some of the sociohistorical processes underlying Nazi thinking and behavior. Rather than questioning the authenticity of the motivations behind Nazi animal protection—a question that is unanswerable—it may be more useful to ask how such thinking was possible and what significance it had. Boundary work—the drawing and blurring of lines of demarcation between humans and animals—was essential to the Nazi paradox. After briefly discussing the extent of Nazi animal protection, we will see that this boundary work was effected in three ways—by morally elevating animals, identifying with them, and animalizing humans.

Nazi Animal Protection

Around the end of the nineteenth century, kosher butchering and vivisection were the foremost concerns of the animal protection movement in Germany. These concerns persisted during the Third Reich and became formalized as laws (Hoelscher 1949; Neff 1989; Trohler and Maehle 1987). In 1927, a Nazi representative to the Reichstag called for measures against cruelty to animals and against kosher butchering (Meyer 1993). In 1932, a ban on vivisection was proposed by the Nazi party (Schröder 1976), and early in 1933, the Nazi representatives to the Prussian parliament met to enact this ban (Proctor 1988). On April 21, 1933, almost immediately after the Nazis came to power, the parliament passed a set of laws regulating the slaughter of animals. In August 1933, Hermann Göring announced an end to the "unbearable torture and suffering in animal experiments" and threatened to "commit to concentration camps those who still think they can continue to treat animals as inanimate property" (Göring 1939). He decried the "cruel" experiments of unfeeling scientists whose allegedly unanesthetized animals were operated on, burned, or frozen. A ban on vivisection was enacted in Bavaria as well as Prussia (AMA 1933), but the Nazis then established a partial ban, a retreat which provoked some criticism within the Nazi movement (Giese and Kahler 1944).

The Nazi animal protection laws of November 1933 permitted experiments on animals in some circumstances, but subject to a set of eight conditions and only with the explicit permission of the Minister of the Interior, supported by the recommendation of local authorities. The conditions were designed to eliminate pain and prevent unnecessary experiments. Horses, dogs, cats, and apes were singled out for special protection. Permission to experiment on animals was not given to individuals but only to institutions.

Inconspicuously buried in the 1933 animal protection laws (point four, section two) was a provision for the "mercy killing" of animals. The law not only allowed, but actually required that old, sick, and worn out domesticated animals, for whom "life has become a torment," be "painlessly" put to death. The wording of the provision was ambiguous; it was not entirely clear whether a family would be required to kill, say, an old dog which did nothing but sit by the fire. One binding commentary, passed immediately after the laws themselves, mandated that an expert should decide whether further life for an animal was a "torment" in unclear cases (Giese and Kahler 1944).

In addition to the laws against vivisection and kosher slaughter, other legal documents regulating the treatment of animals were enacted from 1933 through 1943, probably several times the number promulgated in the previous half-century (Giese and Kahler 1944). These documents covered in excruciating detail a vast array of concerns, from the shoeing of horses to the use of anesthesia. One law passed in 1936 showed "particular solicitude" about the suffering of lobsters and crabs (Waite 1977), stipulating that restaurants were to kill crabs, lobsters, and other crustaceans by throwing them one at a time into rapidly boiling water (Giese and Kahler 1944). Several "high officials" had debated the question of the most humane death for lobsters before this regulation was passed, and two officials in the Interior Ministry had prepared a scholarly treatise on the subject (Waite 1977).

Living with Contradiction

The Nazis also sought to protect wildlife. In 1934 and 1935, the focus of Nazi humane legislation shifted from farm animals and pets to creatures of the wild. The preface to the hunting laws of March 27, 1935, announced a eugenic purpose behind the legislation, stating, "The duty of a true hunter is not only to hunt but also to nurture and protect wild animals, in order that a more varied, stronger and healthier breed shall emerge and be preserved" (Giese and Kahler 1944). A uniform national hunting association was created to regulate the sport, restock lakes, tend forests, and protect dying species (Proctor 1988). Taxes levied on hunters were to be used for upkeep of forests and game parks. Nazi veterinary journals often featured reports on endangered species. Göring, in particular, was concerned about the near extinction in Germany of bear, bison, and wild horses and he sought to establish conservation and breeding programs for dwindling species. He also established three nature reserves, reared forty-seven bison, and created a game research laboratory where he reintroduced the night owl, wood grouse, heathcock, gray goose, raven, beaver, and otter (Irving 1989).

In many respects, the laws of November 1933 were not so very different from the laws protecting animals in Britain, then considered to be the most comprehensive in the world. The severity of the punishments mandated by the German laws was, however, virtually unprecedented in modern times. "Rough mistreatment" of an animal could lead to two years in prison plus a fine (Giese and Kahler 1944). It is not clear, however, how vigorously or conscientiously the animal protection laws were enforced, particularly outside Prussia. Like virtually all legal documents, these laws contained ambiguities and possible loopholes. Neal Barnard (1990), for instance, maintains that several experiments on animals were conducted secretly by Nazi doctors. And Raul Hilberg (1961) describes several Nazi medical experiments on animals that preceded those on human beings. At any rate, Nazi Germany gradually became a state where petty theft could result in death while violent crimes might go unpunished; punishment did not fit the crime in any traditional sense. The new government retained the entire legal apparatus of the Weimar Republic, but used it in the service of a different concept. In accordance with declarations by Adolf Hitler, for example, the laws of July 2, 1934, on "measures for protection of the state" provided that punishment was to be determined not by the crime itself but by the "fundamental idea" behind the crime (Staff 1964). Mistreatment of animals, then might be taken by courts as evidence of a fundamentally antisocial mentality or even of Jewish blood.

It is doubtful whether there was a single, major driving force behind these laws, since the motives of the Nazis, like those of other people, were often contradictory and confusing. For some, there may have been a genuine concern for animals. After all, the objective of the laws was to minimize pain, according to one doctoral dissertation on animal protection written in Germany primarily during the Nazi period (Hoelscher 1949).

For others, the Nazi animal protection laws, formulated with considerable medical and legal sophistication, may have reflected bureaucratic thoroughness and an impulse toward centralization of power that would regulate all relationships. This certainly occurred in relation to animal protection groups. Thus, a decree of August 11, 1938, provided for the merger of various organizations devoted to animal protection, and they were combined in a single bureaucracy under the Ministry of the Interior. All local organizations that resisted the merger were abolished. Membership in the umbrella organization called the Riechs-Tierschutzverein (Association for the Protection of Animals of the Reich) was confined to persons of "Germanic or related blood," and the organization was empowered to monitor and censure activities that could, in the view of the leadership, "place animal protection in jeopardy" (Giese and Kahler 1944, 138).

But this attempt to control relationships seems also to have extended to human behavior toward animals. In their desire to achieve conformity and to control everything, the Nazis may have sought to require humane attitudes. The purpose of the law for the protection of animals, as noted in its introduction, was "to awaken and strengthen compassion as one of the highest moral values of the German people" (Giese and Kahler 1944, 139).

Another possible force behind the animal protection measures may have been changing attitudes toward crime and guilt that called for the protection of things deemed of value to the Nazi state. That animals were to be protected for their own sakes rather than for their relationship to humanity was a new legal concept (Giese and Kahler 1944). By the same token, since Jews were useless to Germany, there was no reason to enact laws to protect them (Bookbinder 1993).

According to Helmut Meyer (1993), two additional forces may have accounted for the rapid passage of the animal protection laws. Accidental circumstances, such as Hitler's personal contact with the veterinarian Dr. F. Weber, an opponent of kosher slaughter, may have been a factor. A more important force, Meyer contends, was the need for the Nazis in 1933 to secure and consolidate their power by obtaining acclaim from broad segments of the population. Perhaps they hoped that the passage of animal protection laws would improve their image by demonstrating their humanitarianism and eliciting approval from Germans as well as foreigners.

Preoccupation with animal protection in Nazi Germany continued almost until the end of World War II. In 1934, the new government hosted an international conference on animal protection in Berlin. Over the speakers' podium, surrounded by enormous swastikas, were the words "Entire epochs of love will be needed to repay animals for their value and service" (Meyer 1975). In 1936, the German Society for Animal Psychology was founded, and in 1938 animal protection was accepted as a subject to be studied in German public schools and universities. In 1943, an academic program in animal psychology was inaugurated at the Hanover School of Veterinary Medicine (Giese and Kahler 1944).

Moral Elevation

Though it appeared politically monolithic, the Nazi movement contained a surprisingly wide range of intellectual opinions. The leaders, in general, showed little interest in abstract theory, and only

Alfred Rosenberg attempted to synthesize Nazism into a cohesive set of doctrines. One cannot, therefore, understand the movement as though it were centered on an abstract philosophy, searching for more formal kinds of logic and coherence. Nazism was far more a cluster of loosely associated concerns. Even leading National Socialists avoided committing themselves on the subject of ideology, emphasizing that in its totality, National Socialism was indefinable (Fest 1970).

Nevertheless, the National Socialists attempted to actualize a racial ideology and, in so doing, create a new Germanic identity (Mosse 1966). The search for the German national character certainly did not start during the Third Reich. The enormous anxiety and preoccupation of the Nazis over national identity and differentiation from other human groups was only a heightened version of Germany's long obsession with its identity and its boundaries with other human groups and animals. Essential to this construction of national identity was the blurring of boundaries between humans and animals as well as with nature more generally that were articulated in German romantic poetry, music, and social thought. These ideas shaped Nazi thinking and served as intellectual resources that were drawn upon and distorted when expedient.

Cult Worship of Animals

One influential theme, particularly evident in the work of Friedrich Nietzsche, was the rejection of intellectual culture and the embrace of animal instinct in humans. This view celebrated the earth and animals in mythical ways and glorified the blond-haired beast who purified the race by copulation. With its qualities of vitality, unscrupulousness, and obedience (Glaser 1978), Nietzsche's *"Raubtier"* (beast of prey), or "blond beast," glorified the animal origin and character of humans.

Nietzsche was one of several heroes whose work was distorted under Nazism to become more brutal and aggressive, particularly his conception of the "blond beast." Hermann Glaser calls this element of National Socialism "man as predator." "The domestic animal who had been domesticated only on the surface was in the end superior to and more honest than man; in the predator, one could rediscover his instincts and with that, his honesty" (Glaser 1978, 138). Animal instinct came to represent rebellion against culture and intellectualism. Returning to the animal nature within humans, communing with nature, and elevating animal life to the level of cult worship were seen as alternatives to modernity, technology, and urbanization, according to Glaser. Acceptance of this view, it was thought, would lead to spiritual and ideological changes necessary and desirable for a new national self-identity to emerge in German cultural life (Gasman 1971).

Indeed, many Nazi leaders called for a return to the pre-Christian tribal mentality of barbarian hunters who worshiped nature and held animals in awe. The barbarian, according to advocates of this view such as Hermann Göring, was much closer to the stag, elk, and wild boar than to the financier or the teacher. As Göring proclaimed, "Yes, we are barbarians, and we think with our blood" (Bookbinder 1993, 75).

As part of the rejection of modern intellectualized culture, the new German, according to National Socialist ideology, was to disavow humanitarian behavior toward fellow humans as insincere. One element of this totalitarian system was the principle of contempt for certain human beings. Heinrich Himmler, for example, called for renouncing "softness" (Fest 1970). "False" comradeship and compassion were derogated. Instead of encouraging compassion, Hitler emphasized that the new German should emulate certain animal behaviors, such as the obedience and faithfulness of pets and the strength, fearlessness, aggressiveness, and even cruelty, supposedly found in beasts of prey—qualities that were highly prized by the movement (Fest 1970).

The training of SS personnel, the Nazi elite guard, illustrated the importance of these animal qualities, even if it ironically meant killing animals. According to Glenn Radde (1991), an oral historian of Nazi Germany, after twelve weeks of working closely with a German shepherd, each SS soldier had to break his dog's neck in front of an officer in order to earn his stripes. Doing so, it was thought, would instill teamwork, discipline, and obedience to the Führer— qualities that were deemed more important than feelings for anything else, including animals.

Hitler himself pleaded for these qualities in German youth: "I want violent, imperious, fearless, cruel young people. . . . The free, magnificent beast of prey must once again flash from their eyes. I want youth strong and beautiful, . . . and athletic youth. . . . In this way I shall blot out thousands of years of human domestication. I shall have the pure, noble stuff of nature" (Maltitz 1973). In another instance, Hitler called for German youth to be as "swift as whippets" (Grunberger 1971). The new Germans were to be part animal while renouncing a part of their humanity. The model German would identify with animals and display the supposed cold aggressiveness of animal instinct. The compassion normally reserved for humans was to be redirected toward animals. This was, in fact, part of the intent of the animal protection laws.

Animals as Moral Beings

A second theme was that animals were to be regarded as moral, if not sacred, beings. For example, the German zoologist Ernst Haeckel, writing at the turn of the century, attacked religion, primarily Christianity, for putting humans above animals and nature; religion had isolated humans from nature and thus evoked contempt for animals. He believed that humans and animals had the same natural as well as moral status and that much of human morality stemmed from animals, claiming that Christian moral principles, such as "Do unto others as you would have them do unto you," were "derived from our animal ancestors" (Bramwell 1989, 49).

In Haeckel's view, animals were to be learned from and the laws of nature used as a guide to reform human societies. The function of human societies, like animal societies, was survival, and biological fitness was essential to both of them. Not surprisingly, Haeckel supported "racial hygiene" through euthanasia. He deduced the ideal state from his observations of animals and nature, maintaining that the most efficient organization to ensure survival among animals was one characterized by a high degree of centralization and hierarchy, like the brain and nervous system, and therefore human society should adopt such an organization, too. In his analyses, Haeckel stressed "duty" as essential to the success of an ideal society. Duty, he claimed, was a biological impulse shared with all animals who were bound to care for family and the larger collectivity because both were necessary for survival (Bramwell 1989).

Haeckel's views informed the Nazi outlook toward animals as moral beings. Religion was also blamed for the attitude that assigned animals to a lower moral status and thereby justified their use by humans. Because there was actually little difference between humans and animals, Germans had a humanitarian duty to animals, as pronounced in the following Nazi propaganda statement:

> Most Germans were brought up with a notion that God created animals to benefit humans. . . . In general, they [clergymen] merely intend to make the difference between humans and the soulless animal appear as large as possible. Every friend of animals knows the extent of mutual understanding between humans and animals and the feeling of community that can develop. (Wuttke-Groneberg 1980, 321)

The Nazis called for redressing wrongs to animals; humans were to have a regard for nature as a moral duty. Joseph Goebbels commented in his diaries: "Man should not feel so superior to animals. He has no reason to. Man believes that he alone has intelligence, a soul, and the power of speech. Has not the animal these things? Just because we, with our dull senses, cannot recognize them, it does not prove that they are not there" (Goebbels 1983, 77).

The moral status of animals was to be changed in the coming German empire: these sentient beings would be accorded love and respect as a sacred and essential element in man's relationship with nature. For example, toward the end of World War II, the editors of a book on the legal protection of animals proclaimed, "Animals are not, as before [the Nazi period], objects of personal property or unprotected creatures, with which a man may do as he pleases, but pieces of living nature which demand respect and compassion." Looking to the future, they quoted the words of Göring that, "for the protection of animals, the education of humanity is more important than laws" (Giese and Kahler 1944, 274).

Society was not to violate animals by killing them, either for sport or for food. The vision of the future was a world where animals would not be unnecessarily harmed. Hunting became a symbol of the civilization left behind; meat-eating became a symbol of the decay of other civilizations; and vegetarianism became a symbol of the new, pure civilization that was to be Germany's future. Hunting was seen as appropriate to an earlier stage of humanity when killing animals involved some "risk" to the hunter. Now, only "sick" animals and those needed for food should be killed. When animals were to be killed for food, they should be given a "sacred" status and their death seen as a form of "sacrifice." This spiritual attitude toward animals, even when they must be killed, could be discerned in Nazi farm propaganda:

> The Nordic peoples accord the pig the highest possible honor . . . in the cult of the Germans the pig occupies the first place and is the first among the domestic animals. . . . The predominance of the pig, the sacred animal destined to sacrifices among the Nordic peoples, has drawn its originality from the great trees of the German forest. (Brady 1969, 53)

Unity of Nature and Humans

A third theme, expressed most vehemently by the composer Richard Wagner in essays as well as music, exalted synthesis against analysis, unity and wholeness against disintegration and atomism, and *Volk* legend against scientific truth (Viereck 1965). Life, in this view, had an organic unity and connection that should not be destroyed by theoretical analysis or physical dissection. Science, and the Jews behind it, was portrayed as destructive intellectualism that treated nature and animals mechanically by dissolving the whole into parts, thereby losing the invisible force that makes the whole more than the sum of its parts.

Wagner's thinking was particularly influential; he had urged smashing laboratories and removing scientists and "vivisectors." The vivisector, to Wagner, came to represent both the scientists' "torture" of animals and the capitalists' torture of the proletariat. He was not alone in portraying the vivisector as both evil and Jewish. In *Gemma, oder Tugend und Laster* (Gemma, or Virtue and Vice), a sentimental novel of the 1870s that did much to arouse public sentiment against animal experimentation, the author portrayed the vivisectionists as cultists who, under the pretense of practicing science, ritualistically cut up living animals in orgiastic rites (Melena 1877). The author may not have intended to identify the vivisectionists in the novel with the Jews (membership in the cult of vivisectionists was a matter of volition rather than heredity), but the representation of vivisectionists in the book was so close to the popular stereotype of Jews engaged in kosher butchering that the connection was unavoidable.

Such views helped to shape the Third Reich's criticisms of scientific thinking and such practices as vivisection. The path of Western civilization had taken an incorrect turn, according to National Socialism. Mechanistic, exploitative technology, attributed to the Jews and to "science," was seen as disconnecting humans from nature and ultimately their own spirit. It became important to portray German leaders as close to nature and having values compatible with a simple agricultural way of life; the soil was seen as the source of life and inspiration. Old Germans, Himmler argued, were nature worshipers, and so, too, should new Germans be; he tried to sell them on the nobility and virtues of farm life (Deuel 1942). Companionship with dogs, in particular, was supposed to forge a link between the soil and humanity. One propaganda photo showed Hitler and "two friends" (two dogs), and another showed Hitler relaxing with a dog (Maltitz 1973; Toland 1976). A great deal was written about Hitler's "modesty and simplicity," which, according to Walter Langer, were the key values behind rural glorification (Langer 1972).

Biological Purity

A fourth theme involved Nordic racism and the biological purity of Aryans. The human race, Nazis argued, had become contaminated and impure through a mixing of the races and the eating of animal flesh. "Regeneration of the human race" was linked to animal protection and vegetarianism. Wagner's principal concern was with the biological purification of Germany and its political future. He believed that socialists had to ally with vegetarians, animal protectionists, and friends of temperance to save mankind from Jewish aggression. Peter Viereck (1965, 119) refers to this "fellowship" as Wagner's "united front of purifiers" who could oppose the antivegetarian stance of Jews. According to Wagner, "The Jewish God found Abel's fatted lamb more savory than Cain's offer" of a vegetable (Viereck 1965, 119).

In an essay, entitled "Heldentum und Christenheit" (Heroism and Christianity), Wagner articulated an anti-Semitic theory of history, which linked vegetarianism to Germany's future (Wagner 1888a). It drew on the racial theories of Joseph Arthur Gobineau, the philosophy of Arthur Schopenhauer, and Wagner's own idiosyncratic brand of Catholicism. Wagner believed that, in abandoning their original vegetarian diet, people had become corrupted by the blood of slaughtered animals. This degeneration was then spread by the mixing of races. Interbreeding eventually spread through the entire Roman Empire, until only the "noble" Germanic race remained pure. After their conquest of Rome, the Germans, however, finally succumbed by mating with the subject peoples. "Regeneration" could be achieved, even by highly corrupted races such as the Jews, through a return to natural foods, provided this was accompanied by partaking of the Eucharist. Wagner also believed that one could not live without "animal food" in the northern climates, so he suggested that in the future there would be a German migration to warmer climates where it would not be necessary to eat animals, thereby permitting Europe to return to pristine jungle and wild beasts (Viereck 1965).

Racial contamination, some argued, had mixed biologically inferior human stock with Aryan blood, thereby threatening the purity of the highest species. The physician Ludwig Woltmann, for example, described the Germans as the highest species because of their perfect physical proportions and their heightened spirituality (Woltmann 1936). He argued that the Germans' life was a constant struggle against the subhuman, which threatened the biological decay of this highest species. This notion can be linked to an intellectual undercurrent in the German movement known as the neo-Manichaean gnosis, a third-century cosmology given a secular form by a defrocked Viennese monk at the beginning of the twentieth century. The former monk, Adolf Lanz, who adopted the name Baron von Liebenfels, published a book called *Theozoology,* in which he claimed that in the beginning there were two races, the Aryans and the Apes or the "animal people." The Aryans were pure and good; the animal people represented darkness and sought to defile Aryans sexually. Interbreeding had obliterated the original races, but Lanz claimed that one could still distinguish and rank races according to the proportion of Aryan or ape blood they possessed. Thus, Nordic people were close to pure Aryan and their racial rank was the highest, while Jews ranked the lowest because they were close to pure ape (Rhodes 1980).

Lanz published a pulp magazine entitled *Ostara, Briefbucher der Blonden Mannesrechtler* (Newsletters of the Blond Fighters for Male Rights), in which all of history was explained in lurid terms as a struggle between the noble Aryan and the hairy subhuman, as the latter continually sought to contaminate the "higher" race by leading blond beauties astray. He founded an organization called the New Templars, which adopted the swastika as its banner. As a young man, Hitler read *Ostara* and may have met several times with Lanz (Sklar 1977, 17). Similar ideas appeared in the writings of Wagner, who maintained in "Heldentum" that the Semitic races had always viewed themselves as descended from the apes, while the Aryan races traced their descent "from the Gods" (Wagner 1888a).

The Nazis, in many ways, departed from the anthropocentric understanding of the cosmos that dominated Occidental civilization since at least the late Middle Ages. Nazi thinking was centered on the process of evolution, conceived as a process of perpetual improvement through "survival of the fittest." This process, however, was not viewed as a spontaneous process but as something that, in the contemporary world, sometimes required assistance (Proctor 1988). In other words, it became a project to perfect biologically what it meant to be German—a task not unlike that taken with German shepherd dogs, who were deliberately bred to represent and embody the spirit of National Socialism. Van Stephanitz, the creator of this breed, sought national status for a local population of coyotelike dogs, analogous to the allegedly "superior" bred Aryans, whose only reason for being was to go to war on the day hostilities began (Radde 1991).

One influential theorist of evolutionary progress in the Nazi party was Konrad Lorenz, who viewed the human race as having reached a critical point between extinction and development to a "higher" organism. In an essay published in 1940, Lorenz wrote that "the great decision of today depends on whether we learn to fight the degeneration, in our people and in the entire human race, resulting from a lack of natural selection, before it is too late. Precisely in this decision of survival or extinction we Germans are very far ahead of all other cultural people" (Baümler-Schleinkofer 1990, 54–55).

Central to National Socialist ideology was the quest for racial purity by creating a "superrace" and eliminating "inferior races." Indeed, laws passed under the Third Reich to improve the eugenic stock of animals anticipated the way in which Germans and non-Aryans were treated eugenically. Germans were to be treated as farm animals bred for the most desirable Aryan traits while ridding themselves of weaker and less desirable specimens. Such a remodeling of civilization was not to flout the "natural order," meaning that distinctions among humans, animals, and the larger "natural" world should not make up the basic structure of life. Rather, the fundamental distinction made during the Third Reich was between that which was regarded as "racially" pure and that which was polluting and dangerous. The former was embodied in the Aryan people and nature, the latter in other humans who were equated with "lower" animals.

According to Hitler's own fanciful anthropology, non-Aryans were subhuman and should be considered lower than domestic animals. He stated in *Mein Kampf* that slavery came before the domestication of animals. The Aryans supposedly subjugated the "lower races": "First the vanquished drew the plough, only later the horse" (Hilter 1938, 328). This, in Hitler's imagination, was the "paradise" that the Aryans eventually lost through the "original sin" of mating with the conquered people. The notion of race, as used by the Nazis, in many ways assumed the symbolic significance usually associated with species; the new phylogenetic hierarchy could locate certain "races below animals." The Germans were the highest "species," above all other life; most "higher" animals, however, were above other "races" or "subhumans."

Identification with Animals

Personal

In trying to understand the pairing of apparent concern for animals with cruelty toward humans, we cannot ignore the possibility that these attitudes can coexist in one person. Nazis who advocated humane measures for animals and inhumane acts against humans may have had genuine interest in and affection for animals while simultaneously feeling indifference or hatred for people.

On the one hand, this explanation can be questioned because reports of Nazi compassion for animals are based on historical anecdotes or personal diaries and memoranda that may have been circulated or written to create a sympathetic image of Nazi leaders as warm and humane people or as having values consistent with the National Socialist movement. Norbert Bromberg and Verna Small, for instance, contend that Hitler's compassion for animals was no more sincere than his interest in children; both were mere propaganda ploys. He supposedly once "mercilessly beat a dog in order to appear masculine before a young girl" (Bromberg and Small 1983, 178). Indeed, the following portrayal of Hitler, which appeared in the magazine *Neugeist/die Weisse,* certainly smacks of propaganda:

> Do you know that your Führer is a vegetarian, and that he does not eat meat because of his general attitude toward life and his love for the world of animals? Do you know that your Führer is an exemplary friend of animals, and even as a chancellor, he is not separated from the animals he has kept for years? . . . The Führer is an ardent opponent of any torture of animals, in particular vivisection, and has declared to terminate those conditions . . . thus fulfilling his role as the savior of animals, from continuous and nameless torments and pain. (Wuttke-Groneberg 1980, 81)

Helmut Meyer (1993) argues that prominent Nazis cared about animals when they were personally close to them but not when they were anonymous masses. As an example, he points to Hitler's order to kill thirty-thousand horses at Krim to prevent them from falling into Russian hands. On the other hand, there are reasons to take these accounts seriously. Many of these reports were made before the Nazi rise to power in the 1930s and 1940s, when they were less likely to have served as propaganda, and some were made after the war by psychiatrists conducting assessments of prisoners of war. In addition, these sympathetic attitudes toward animals were consistent with the larger cultural and historical context of German thinking discussed above.

Numerous anecdotal reports suggest that Hitler enjoyed the company of dogs as companion animals. Throughout much of his life, dogs were Hitler's closest attachments (Padfield 1984). For example, Hitler's landlady observed that a large dog named Wolf was his constant companion. John Toland (1976, 133) claims that Hitler "had a need for the faithfulness he found in dogs, and had a unique understanding of them," once commenting that some dogs "are so intelligent that it's agonizing." According to Peter Padfield (1984), Hitler frequently praised his wolfhound Blondi's wholehearted devotion to him, while expressing doubts about the complete loyalty of his staff. Toward the end of the war, Hitler came to depend on the companionship of Eva Braun, Blondi, and her pups (Stone 1980). During his final days in the bomb shelter, Hitler permitted no one but himself to touch or feed Blondi's pup, Wolf (Waite 1977), and he risked his life every day by taking Blondi for a walk outside his bunker (Serpell 1986). When it came time for Hitler and the others to commit suicide, he could not bring himself to give poison to Blondi or watch her die (Payne 1960).

Hitler was not the only prominent Nazi to keep pets. Göring was unusually fond of and dedicated to several pet adult lions kept at his estate. According to David Irving (1989), chief forester Ulrich Scherping claimed that those who saw Göring with his lions could sense the fondness that they had for each other. Goebbels, Rudolph Hess, Rudolph Franz Höss, and several other elite Nazis had pet dogs. A typical case of such affection was that of Karl Dönitz, admiral of the German navy, who was known to have a deep love for dogs. Whenever he returned home, his first greeting was for the family dog. Later, there was another pet dog named Wolf, whom "he loved dearly." He remarked more than once that "there is nothing in the world more faithful than a dog. He believes his master unconditionally. What he does is right" (Padfield 1984, 331). Dönitz also expressed concern for stray dogs: "I think I shall start a kindergarten when I get out, a mixed one for puppies as well as children" (Padfield 1984, 475). He did not, however, ever create such an orphanage. Padfield suggests that Dönitz may have simply fallen under the influence of Hitler, who emphasized the virtues of obedience in animals, or, conversely, had doubts about the correctness of the path he was following. Or perhaps he, like Hitler, had doubts about the complete loyalty of his staff.

As mentioned earlier, the only advocate of hunting was Göring, but as Paul Bookbinder (1993, 78) notes, "The stag that Göring could hunt, who would face him in an honest pitting of wit, strength, and skill in a contest Göring knew he would win, was a creature that Göring preferred to his fellow human beings." Other Nazis showed little interest in or staunchly opposed hunting; Hitler was known to have a strong distaste for it. Toland (1976, 424–425) recounts that once, when dinner conversation turned to hunting, Hitler commented, "I can't see what there is in shooting, you go out armed with a highly perfected modern weapon and without risk to yourself kill a defenseless animal." Hitler frequently criticized hunting as a "remnant" of a "dead feudal world." He remarked, "How can a person be excited about such a thing? Killing animals, if it must be done, is the butcher's business. . . . I understand, of course, that there must be professional hunters to shoot sick animals. If only there were still some danger connected with hunting, as in the days when men used spears for killing game." Himmler also opposed hunting. He had a "positively hysterical opposition" to hunting, and viewed it as "pure murder" of the "innocent" (Speer 1970, 115–116).

Many leading Nazis practiced vegetarianism. Hitler hired a vegetarian cook (Payne 1960, 566) and became very critical of others who were not vegetarian, sometimes referring to beef broth as "corpse tea" and sausage as "cadavers" (Waite 1977, 19). The vegetarianism of other Germans was a fad spawned by Hitler's preferences (Stone 1980, 62). Some became even more fanatic about it than Hitler. Hess was so worried about the food he ate with Hitler in the Chancellery that he would bring his own vegetarian food in containers, defending his practice by saying that his food had to contain "ideologically dynamic ingredients" (Manvell and Fraenkel 1971, 64).

Following Wagner, Hitler believed that eating meat was contaminating, because of the mixture of animal and Aryan blood (Waite, 1977, 64), and that civilization could be regenerated through vegetarianism. Several entries in Goebbels' diaries underscore the notion that Nazis aspired to vegetarianism as a higher state of humanity. In one entry, Goebbels observed that "animals that live on plants have much greater powers of resistance than those that feed on meat" (Goebbels 1948, 188). In another entry, Goebbels noted: "Meat-eating is a perversion of our human nature. When we reach a higher level of civilization, we shall doubtless overcome it" (Goebbels 1983, 6).

Nazis often paired their identification with animals, however, with contempt for humanity. The usual explanation is that many Nazi leaders had difficulty sustaining relationships with other hu-

Living with Contradiction

mans, because the Nazis were socially marginal or alienated. Not surprisingly, they may have found it easier to develop relationships with animals (Bryant 1993). Lifton (1986) suggests that caring for animals may have had more complex psychological roots in serving as a coping device that allowed Nazis to "double," seeing themselves as humane while behaving insensitively or cruelly toward humans. Whatever the motivation, key members of the German general staff may have personally identified with animals while despising humanity.

Most notably, Hitler is often depicted as having contempt for and fear of humans but compassion and warmth for animals. Toland (1976) notes that it became known in the Third Reich that Hitler had a deep affection "for all dumb creatures," but very little for men and women. "It was as though, since the Viennese days, he had turned away from the human race, which had failed to live up to his expectations and was therefore damned. At the heart of the mystery of Hitler was his fear and contempt of people"(p. 425). Similarly, Payne observes that Hitler felt closer to and more compassion for certain animals than people, when it came to their suffering. Payne reports that a German pilot recalled that "Hitler saw films given to him by a friendly Maharaja. During the scenes showing men savagely torn to pieces by animals, he remained calm and alert. When the films showed animals being hunted, he would cover his eyes with his hands and asked to be told when it was all over. Whenever he saw a wounded animal, he wept" (Payne 1960, 461). He hated people who engaged in blood sports, and several times he said it would give him the greatest pleasure to murder anyone who killed an animal.

Similarly, while Goebbels' attitude toward humans was contemptuous, his expressed attitude toward his pet dog was loving. His diary entries, especially those written in the mid-1920s, were explicit about this disjunction in feelings. Goebbels revealed:

As soon as I am with a person for three days, I don't like him any longer; and if I am with him for a whole week, I hate him like the plague.... I have learned to despise the human being from the bottom of my soul. He makes me sick in my stomach. Phoeey!! Much

dirt . . . and many intrigues. . . . The only real friend one has in the
end is the dog. . . . The more I get to know the human species, the
more I care for my Benno [his pet dog]. (Goebbels 1948, 8)

Other members of the German Nazi elite identified with animals
and showed similar loving concern for their pets. Hess was quite
pleased when his pet wolfhound Hasso gave birth to three puppies
(Leasor 1962). Höss, the commander of Auschwitz, was a "great
lover" of animals, particularly horses. After a hard day's work at the
camp, he "found relief walking through the stables at night" (Glaser
1978, 240). Eduard Wirth, a prominent physician at Auschwitz, had
three pet dogs at one point. When two became ill, he referred to one
of his rooms as their "sick ward." When his favorite dog died, he
wrote sadly to his wife of its death, noting that the dog "suffered a
lot so I gave him morphine. . . . It is good that he dies; he was in the
end blind in both eyes" (Lifton 1986, 399).

Psychological assessments of the personalities of several leading
Nazi political figures also show evidence of distancing from humans and interest in animals. In one study, Rorschach tests were ad-
ministered to Nazi prisoners of war (Miale and Selzer 1975). Results
indicated several departures from "normal" test findings, with subjects seeing themselves as animals or subhuman in the Rorschach
more often than controls did. Half the subjects depicted themselves,
or aspects of themselves, as animals (typically unevolved, low-level
bugs, beetles, or insects); six of the subjects also offered portraits
of themselves as subhuman or inhuman figures such as gremlins.
Florence Miale and Michael Selzer (1975) contend that the respondents' animal responses lacked vitality, indicating that the
members of this group were "cut off from their vital impulses and
were unable to be free and spontaneous. Their antisocial attitudes
were not expressions of normal impulses, but rather of the repres-
sion and distortion of these impulses"(p. 276). In short, the findings
suggested that, on the whole, these men had an "incapacity to feel
human feelings"(p. 232). Henry Dicks (1972) also found that the
Nazis he studied lacked affectionate and positive intimate human
relationships.

Political

National Socialist propaganda often portrayed Germany as a woman at one with nature but exploited and possessed by demonic Bolsheviks, capitalists, and Jews (Fest 1975; Lane and Rupp 1978). These victimizers were seen as endangering the purity of the German "blood" and "spirit." Animals, too, were being victimized by these oppressors, whether by slaughtering them according to kosher law or by using them as subjects in scientific experiments. Metaphorically, only a subtle difference separated the animal from the German victim in this struggle. The hated "vivisectors" became synonymous with the Jews, enemies of both animals and Germans.

Animal protection measures may have served as a legal vehicle to express these anti-Semitic feelings. This is not to argue that all of these measures were part of a well-defined and orchestrated master plan. But as German law was recast to embody Nazi values, it is reasonable to think that some animal protection measures might have expressed animosity toward certain human groups. And as a totality, these animal protection efforts, at the least, provided an opportunity for attacking various segments of society (Bryant 1993).

Clearly, the banning of kosher slaughter was a deliberate action to isolate the "Jewish disease" through legal means (Lerner 1992). Laws passed by the Nazis on April 21, 1933, to regulate butchering constituted a barely concealed attack on the Jews, whose "ritualistic slaughter" was characterized as "torment of animals." The preamble to the laws stated:

> The animal protection movement, strongly promoted by the National Socialist government, has long demanded that animals be given anesthesia before being killed. The overwhelming majority of the German people have long condemned killing without anesthesia, a practice universal among Jews though not confined to them . . . as against the cultivated sensitivities of our society. (Giese and Kahler 1944)

The discussion that followed contained further references to the horrors allegedly found in kosher butcher shops.

The German movement against animal experimentation was also, from its inception, strongly associated with anti-Semitism. In a decree issued on August 17, 1933, Göring declared:

> I . . . will commit to concentration camps those who still think they can continue to treat animals as inanimate property. . . . The fairy tales and sagas of the Nordic people, especially the German people, show the spirit of close contact, which all Aryan people possess, with the animals. It is the more incomprehensible, therefore, that justice, up to now, did not agree with the spirit of the people on this point as it did on many others. Under the influence of foreign [i.e., Jewish] conceptions of justice . . . the animal was considered a dead thing under their law. (Göring 1939, 70–71)

The statement is particularly noteworthy, since the very existence of concentration camps was generally not acknowledged at the time.

Nazi ideologues sought to link the history of Judaism to vivisection. The revelations of Abraham and Moses were understood as the dominant tradition of the Occident, which culminated in the industrial revolution and the human domination of nature. The word *"vivisektion"* (almost the same in German as in English) was often used broadly to refer to all dispassionate dissection and analysis. Judaism, in both actual and symbolic ways, was understood as the tradition of "vivisection." Nazi racial theorists regularly contrasted the supposedly cold, analytic mentality of the Jew with that of "Nordic man," who, they claimed, comprehended things organically as part of the natural world (Giesler 1938).

The anti-Semitism of the Nazis was a very radical form of an idea that is still familiar: that Jews and, by association, Christians had scorned the natural world. Some of the Nazis, such as chief ideologist Alfred Rosenberg, rejected Christianity as a sect of Judaism, while others tried to purge Christianity of its Jewish heritage and purify it (Mosse 1966). As a result, the distinction between Christianity and paganism in Nazi Germany grew increasingly unclear (Glaser 1978).

The Nazi link between animal protection and anti-Semitism is paradoxical, since the Old Testament celebrates animals with great passion and eloquence. Nevertheless, such an association has a long history in European culture. In the fourteenth century, Geoffrey Chaucer satirized it in his *Canterbury Tales*. When the Prioress is introduced, we are told how well she fed her hounds and how she would weep at the sight of a mouse caught in a trap. But this same Prioress uses her tale to make a furious attack on Jews, accusing them of ritual murder of children (Chaucer 1969). More recently, in the mid-nineteenth century, philosopher Arthur Schopenhauer held that Jewish traditions were responsible for a view of animals as objects (Schopenhauer 1903).

The key figure in promoting this association, however, was Wagner. Long after he died, his writings continued to have considerable impact on German thought. He dramatized his ideas respecting race and animal protection in the opera *Parsifal,* and his prose sometimes contains blood imagery that constantly appears in the later rhetoric of Hitler and his followers (Craige 1992). In a letter of August 1879 to Ernst von Weber, the founder of the Dresden Animal Protection Society and author of the influential *Die Folterkammern der Wissenschaft* (The Torture Chambers of Science), Wagner stated:

> One must begin by drawing people's attention to animals and reminding them of the Brahman's great saying "Tat twam asi" (that art thou)—even though it will be difficult to make it acceptable to the modern world of Old Testament Judaization [the spread of Jewish blood and influence]. However, a start must be made here—since the commandment to love thy neighbor is becoming more and more questionable and difficult to observe—particularly in the face of our vivisectionist friends. (Wagner 1987, 896)

Like Göring and others who would come later, Wagner identified vivisectionists with Jews.

A much-expanded version of the above letter was published that October under the title "Offenes Schreiben an Ernst von Weber" (Open Letter to Ernst von Weber). The revision was even more emotional in tone. Wagner supported breaking into laboratories where experiments on animals were conducted, as well as physical attacks on vivisectionists. He closed with the melodramatic declaration that, should the campaign against vivisection prove unsuccessful, he would gladly depart from a world in which dogs would no longer wish to live (Wagner 1888b). With Wagner's public and financial support and von Weber's skillful leadership, the Dresden Animal Protection Society soon became the center of the German antivivisection movement (Trohler and Maehle 1987).

As illustrated by the quotation from Wagner's original letter, anti-Semitic rhetoric in Germany suggested that persecution of Jews was sometimes put forward as revenge on behalf of aggrieved animals. Jews were identified as enemies of animals and implicitly of Germans. In Wagner's outrage against the use of frogs in experiments, he explicitly identified "vivisectors" as "enemies" and vivisection of frogs as "the curse of our civilization." Wagner urged the *Volk* to rid itself of scientists and rescue the frog–martyrs. Viereck (1965, 108) maintains that Wagner created a "sort of moral Armageddon" between those "who free trussed animals" and those "who truss them to torture them." Those who fail to untruss frogs were "enemies of the state."

After the death of Wagner in 1883, his followers, among them the brothers Bernard and Paul Forstner, continued the anti-Semitic campaign against vivisection. The latter became editor of *Thier-und Menschenfreund* (Friend to Animals and Humans), the journal of the Dresden Animal Protection Society. Wagner's admirers in the twentieth century included such spokesmen for anti-Semitism as Houston Stewart Chamberlain, Alfred Rosenberg, and most significantly, Adolf Hitler (Katz 1986).

Another close associate of von Weber who added prestige to the movement against vivisection was Friedrich Zöllner, a famous though controversial professor of astrophysics (Bretschneider 1962). In a popular book entitled *Über den Wissenschaftlichen Missbrauch der Vivisektion* (On the Scientific Misuse of Vivisection), first published in 1880, Zöllner launched an attack against physiologists. For example, he attacked a Jewish zoologist named Semper, accusing him of showing gross insensitivity (a "thick skin" like that of an elephant) by hunting the birds that attacked his botanical gardens, with the following sarcastic remarks:

> One would be justified in describing the anti-Semitic movement not as "persecution of Jews," but metaphorically as a "hunt for elephants." Because surely Professor Semper would recognize a right to hunt not only thrushes but also elephants if they broke into his garden. The German people have the same right to hunt educated, Semitic "elephants" as Semper does to hunt the thrushes. (Zöllner 1885, 89)

The reversal of roles between hunter and animal is an old motif that appears frequently in literature against misuse of animals (Sax 1990).

Although Zöllner did not unequivocally advocate physical attacks on Jews, this passage is an anticipation of Nazi persecutions. Despite what this quotation suggests, Zöllner seems to have been far less a vicious man than a complacent one. Confident that concern for animals proved his moral superiority, he could, elsewhere in his book, content himself with the most abstract expressions of compassion for the Jews. Many of his attitudes were later adopted by Nazi doctors who attempted to purify medicine of "Jewish" influence (Proctor 1988).

Animalization of Humans

While the Nazis derided mathematics and physics as "Jewish" or "mechanistic," they granted a virtually unprecedented prestige to biology and medicine. These latter fields, in turn, acquired the sort of mystical overtones that are frequently associated with the most abstract disciplines. National Socialists looked to biology for ultimate answers, not only to questions of cause and effect but to ethical ones as well.

This medicalization of moral and aesthetic issues, far from being an aberration, had a basis in traditions going back for centuries and included some of the most illustrious names in German culture. It may be found, for example, in Goethe's famous remark to Johann

Peter Eckermann that classicism is the art of health while romanticism is that of disease. The notion was made still more explicit in Friedrich Schiller's essay "On Naive and Sentimental Poetry." Later thinkers such as Nietzsche and Thomas Mann broadened the concepts of "disease" and "health" until these terms appeared more metaphysical than scientific.

Guidelines for high school teachers during the Nazi period quoted the statement of Hans Schlemm that "National Socialism is politically applied biology" (Baümer-Schleinkofer 1990, 57–58). Konrad Lorenz observed that "the most deeply committed and passionate National Socialists" were those who had most thoroughly internalized evolutionary theory (Baümer-Schleinkofer 1990, 55). Lifton (1986, 17) has characterized Nazi Germany as a "biocracy," a state in which biological theory was elevated to the status of a religion.

Biological distinctions among people, in consequence, assumed a nearly absolute importance. In accord with a philosophy that equated biology with destiny, institutions such as schools were strictly divided along lines of gender (Koonz 1987). Homosexuality, since it suggested an ambiguous area between the two genders, was strictly forbidden by the Nazis. Nazi society, in other words, was intended to be strictly compartmentalized along biological lines. The actual practice, however, often contradicted this ideal, as official art featured homoerotic themes (Mosse 1966) and leaders such as Hitler appealed to values derided as "feminine" (Koonz 1987).

While stressing the biological distinctions among types of human beings, the Nazis saw human life as part of the larger biological order that they sought to create. As part of this order, all humans, including Germans, were to be treated as animals. Germans were regarded as livestock to breed the purest biological forms; non-Aryans were viewed as pests that could contaminate the racial purity so important to National Socialist aims. This categorization of humans as animals was another reason the combination of animal protection measures with cruelty toward humans may not have seemed paradoxical to Germans. By animalizing human life, moral distinctions between people and animals were obliterated, making it possible to treat animals as considerately as humans and humans as poorly as animals.

Living with Contradiction

In *Der Mythus des 20 Jahrhunderts,* a book intended to have virtually scriptural authority within the Nazi movement, Alfred Rosenberg observed that more concern was shown about the pedigree of horses and donkeys than about that of human beings (Rosenberg 1935). To correct this, the National Socialists would treat Germans themselves, in the most literal sense, as animals. Just as the breeding stock of "less pure" animals had been improved, so, too, was the "pure blood" of Germans to be restored. According to Richard Darre, the Minister of Agriculture, "As we have restored our old Hanoverian horse from less pure male and female animals by selective breeding, we will also, in the course of generations, again selectively breed the pure type of the Nordic German from the finest German bloodlines" (Glaser 1978, 154).

Several leading Germans used their experience in farming, as well as their training in agriculture and veterinary medicine, to pursue this goal. For example, Martin Bormann, often considered second in rank only to Hitler, had been an agricultural student and, in 1920, became the manager of a large farm (McGovern 1968). The rector of the University of Berlin in the mid-1930s was by profession a veterinarian. He instituted twenty-five new courses in *Rassenkunde*—racial science—and, by the time he finished revamping the curriculum, had instituted eighty-six veterinary courses applied to humans (Shirer 1960). And for a period in the 1920s, Himmler was a chicken breeder (Fest 1970). Veterinary medicine and agricultural science became the means of teaching racial doctrine in German universities (Bendersky 1985). Indeed, National Socialism viewed Europe, including Germany, "as if it were a thoroughly neglected animal farm which urgently needed the elimination of racially poor and unhealthy stock, better breeding methods, etc. All of Europe and the East were finally to make biological sense" (Maltitz 1973, 289).

Much of Himmler's knowledge about animal breeding practices was directly applied to plans for human breeding to enhance Aryan traits (Bookbinder 1989). Himmler was obsessed with *Lebensborn* (Spring of Life), his program for breeding superior Nordic offspring (Shirer 1960), although contrary to his racial beliefs, he was willing to use blue-eyed, blond-haired children of murdered Jews to breed from (Gittleman 1993). Financial awards were made for giving birth to a child of biological and racial value, and potential mothers of good Aryan stock who did not bear children were branded as "unwholesome, traitors and criminals" (Deuel 1942, 164–165). The propagation of good German blood was seen as so important that several Nazi leaders advocated free love in special recreation camps for girls with pure Aryan qualities. In one of Himmler's schemes, he argued for establishing 100 such camps, each for 1,000 girls, so that 10,000 "perfect" children would be born each year (Deuel 1942, 165).

Despite the criticism of the Reichminister of the Interior, who opposed the "idea of breeding Nordics" when it reached the point of "making a rabbit-breeding farm out of Germany" (Deuel 1942, 203), plans were developed for a series of state-run brothels where young women certified as genetically sound would be impregnated by Nazi men. The intent was to breed Aryans as if they were pedigreed dogs (Glaser 1978). But since, from the eugenic point of view, a weak animal would probably be of little use no matter how good the stock, the infants of the young German women bred with specially selected "good" German male stock were taken away immediately and "exposed," or put outside, unprotected, to see if they would survive (Gailey 1990).

Other proposals and policies reflected a similar view of the German people as livestock to be improved through proper breeding. Laws passed to regulate marriage were based on "racial blood"; the goal was to prevent contamination of Germanic blood so that children born in Germany would be either purely Jewish or purely non-Jewish (Deuel 1942). Even selection for membership in certain Nazi organizations, such as Himmler's SS, emphasized pure Aryan qualities. To draw the sons of the best genetic families into Nazi ranks, preference was given to those applicants having a certified family tree extending back five or six generations, who had blond hair, blue eyes, and a height of at least six feet. They were to become the biological elite, the purest Germans (Bayles 1940). One proposal suggested sending biologically unfit Germans into battle so that biologically superior individuals could be preserved for reproduction (Gasman 1971).

Medical research under the Third Reich also approached Germans as livestock. For instance, those familiar with Josef Mengele's concentration camp experiments believed that his indifference to the suffering of his victims stemmed from his passion for creating a genetically pure superrace "as though you were breeding horses" (Posner and Ware 1986, 31). The principal purposes of his experiments were to discover the secret of creating multiple births of babies with genetically engineered Aryan features and to improve the fertility of German women, as well as to find efficient and easy ways to conduct mass sterilization of "inferior races" (Posner and Ware 1986, 31).

While the German people themselves were dealt with as biological stock or farm animals, certain groups of people, considered a threat to German blood and culture, were viewed as "lower animals" to be dispatched accordingly. In discussing the goal of selecting out "inferior" races from the world's breeding stock, the language is full of references to contamination from contact with others considered dirty or polluting. Hitler referred to race "poisoning," while others used such terms as "race defilement," "corruption," "decay," "rot," or "decomposition" of German "blood" (Weinstein 1980, 136) to refer to everything from casual acquaintanceship to sexual relations with Jews (Deuel 1942) or contact with their "harmful animal semen" (Brady 1969, 53). Even animals owned by Jews were seen as racially contaminating to other animals. Viereck cites the case of a German mayor who decreed that, in order to further race purity, "Cows and cattle which were [acquired] from Jews, directly or indirectly, may not be bred with the community bull" (Viereck 1965, 254).

Those deemed genetically contaminating were thought of and treated as animals. Such labeling of people, typically emphasizing beastly or wild instincts, was not confined to Jews. "Foreign workers" were "pigs, dogs, they are creatures who are the counterfeits of human beings" (Grunberger 1971, 166). An SS propaganda booklet, "The Subhuman," described all peoples of the "East" as "animalistic trash, to be exterminated" (Herzstein 1978, 365). Russian soldiers were a "conglomeration of animals," "unrestrained beasts," and "wild animals" (Maltitz 1973, 61) and had "primitive animality"

(Herzstein 1978, 357). Even the Romanian peasants, allies of the Germans, were described as "miserable pieces of cattle" (Maltitz 1973, 61).

When groups of people, most commonly Jews, were likened to specific animal species, it was usually "lower" animals or life forms, including rodents, reptiles, insects, or germs. Hitler, for instance, called the Jews "malignant bacillus" (Hitler 1938, 334), and Himmler, seeking to help some soldiers cope with having just shot one hundred Jews, told them that "bedbugs and rats have a life purpose . . . but this has never meant that man could not defend himself against vermin" (Hilberg 1961, 219). In one propaganda film, images of rats were superimposed over presumed "degenerate people" such as Jews, and the 1940 film *The Eternal Jew* portrayed Jews as lower than vermin, somewhat akin to the rat—filthy, corrupting, disease-carrying, ugly, and group oriented (Herzstein 1978, 309). Fred Weinstein (1980) reports that because Jews were thought to be like chameleons—able to merge with their surroundings—they were made to wear the yellow Star of David so that innocent Aryans would not be contaminated by unwitting contact. Jews were also likened to "parasites" and "plagues" of insects (Herzstein 1978, 354).

The most extreme form of animalization branded Jews as *Untermenschen,* or subhumans, lower than animals. As described in one SS document:

> The subhuman—that creation of nature, which biologically is seemingly quite identical with the human, with hands, feet, and a kind of brain, with eyes and a mouth—is nevertheless a totally different and horrible creature, is merely an attempt at being man—but mentally and emotionally on a far lower level than any animal. In the inner life of that person there is a cruel chaos of wild uninhibited passions: a nameless urge to destroy, the most primitive lust, undisguised baseness. But the subhuman lived, too. . . . He associated with his own kind. The beast called the beast . . . And this underworld of subhumans found its leader: the eternal Jew! (Maltitz 1973, 61–62)

This was the final twist on the Nazi phylogenetic inversion; Aryans and certain animals symbolized purity and were above hu-

Living with Contradiction

man animals that were a contaminant involving impure "races" and "lower" animal species; the subhumans were below everything. Hitler, in fact, came to believe that Jews, as subhumans, were biologically demonic. He speculated that they descended from beings, which "must have been veritable devils," and that it was only "in the course of centuries" that they had "taken on a human look" through interbreeding with Aryans. As the personification of the devil, Jews, to Hitler, were the main danger to the purity of the Aryan world (Staudinger 1981). Himmler, also buying into the notion of the subhuman, had studies made of the skulls of "Jewish–Bolshevik commissars" in order to arrive at a typological definition of the "subhuman" (Fest 1970).

The conception of certain people as animal-like, when coupled with a desire for racial purity, may have facilitated experimentation on concentration camp inmates as though they were as expendable as laboratory rats. At the Ravensbruck concentration camp for women, hundreds of Polish inmates—the "rabbit girls" they were called—were given gangrenous wounds while others were subjected to "experiments in bone grafting" (Shirer 1960, 979). In some cases, concentration camp inmates were substituted for animals before trials on Germans. For example, in 1941, Himmler approved the use of camp inmates in a sterilization study of a plant extract based on premature findings from research on rodents (Hilberg 1961). More typical were medical experiments on people that had not even been tried on animals. Experimenters such as Mengele referred to camp inmates as human "material" and their body parts as "war materials" (Posner and Ware 1986, 17, 39). At Belsen, staff members viewed their work in terms of how many "pieces of prisoner per day" were handled, and letters from IG Farben's drug research section and Auschwitz camp authorities made reference to "loads" or "consignments" of human guinea pigs (Grunberger 1971, 330).

Conceiving of certain people as animal-like also made it easier to kill them. Those deemed "unfit" or "unworthy" of life were considered "degenerate"; if permitted to breed, they would only contaminate German stock and reduce its physical, mental, and moral purity

(Deuel 1942, 221, 225). Hence, the need for "hygienic prophylaxis" (Herzstein 1978, 66). Jews, in particular, were viewed as "breeders of almost all evil" (Shirer 1960, 250). The expectation was that those humans deemed polluting and dangerous to the race would be eliminated through a program of euthanasia. *Gnadentod* (mercy killing) was for those with "lives not worth living" (Lifton 1986), a notion that is strikingly similar to the 1933 animal protection regulations regarding euthanasia. The first to be given a "mercy death" were incurably insane persons or deformed infants under a 1939 plan which became known as the "euthanasia program" (Hilberg 1961, 561; Peukert 1987). The killing was then extended to older children. Ironically, Jewish children were at first excluded from the "program." According to the bizarre, dreamlike logic of the National Socialists, Jews did not deserve such an "act of mercy" (Proctor 1988).

The Holocaust victims included Jews, Gypsies, alcoholics, homosexuals, criminals, and almost anyone else the regime objected to. Extermination of humans considered to be contaminating extended beyond the killing of millions in concentration camps. By limiting medical and dental care and fostering abortions, the empire envisioned by the Nazis would not facilitate the survival of native populations, such as those in southern Russia. It was a philosophy of utter contempt for and revulsion from those thought of, in Himmler's words, as "these human animals" (Maltitz 1973, 288–289). Speaking to his SS officers, Himmler commented, "We Germans, who are the only ones in the world who have a decent attitude toward animals, will also show a decent attitude toward these human animals, but it would be a crime against our own blood to worry about them" (Maltitz 1973, 41).

This analysis raises a troubling and unsavory contradiction: that in Nazi Germany disregard for human life was coupled with deep concern for animals. This paradox, however, vanishes if the treatment of humans and animals under the Third Reich is placed in a larger context. All societies seek to order and classify human existence by grouping things in terms of shared qualities. According to Mary

Douglas (1966), when something is ambiguous or hard to classify because it confuses or blurs socially constructed categories, it becomes a source of pollution and a danger to society. The containment or elimination of polluting elements is society's effort to organize a conceptually "safe" environment by preserving the integrity of what is deemed pure. Indeed, by containing the danger of pollution, people can further the illusion of their power as they seek to guard the ideal order of society against the dangers that threaten it.

At the core of this dichotomy of purity and danger is a design of society and a definition of what constitutes its boundaries and margins, and "laws of nature" are cited to strengthen the moral code and social rules that define these boundaries. In Nazi Germany, the conception of what it meant to be Aryan, or pure, relied heavily on seeing other groups of people as the societal danger. The Nazis did this by blurring boundaries between humans and animals and by constructing a unique phylogenetic hierarchy that altered conventional Western human–animal distinctions and imperatives.

Although it may seem inconsistent, German identity was not contaminated by seeing itself closely related to animals in moral, if not biological, terms. At times, Germans saw in themselves the "ideal" qualities embodied in animals such as strength, loyalty, and fearlessness. To cope with their greatest threat, the "genetic pollution" of a pure, holistic, natural people, Germans were encouraged to fight for their survival with the same unfeeling determination as any "wild" species of life was said to do. This blurring was also seen in the alliance of Germans with animals against their "oppressors," Jews and others labeled as "vivisectors" and "torturers." In facing a common danger, Germans likened themselves to animals as "victims" and distanced themselves from human "victimizers." Like animals, Germans were also "virtuous" and "innocent." Finally, this blurring was seen in the animalization of Germans themselves. For example, as part of the natural order, Germans of Aryan stock were to be bred like farm stock.

However, non-Aryans were seen as a polluted category precisely because they were animalized humans, or from Douglas' perspective, a freakish mix of the two categories—human and animal. That the animalization of Aryans was not seen as a pollution, while the animalization of non-Aryans was so defined, only points to the capriciousness of socially constructed categories. "Natural," taken-for-granted dichotomies, such as human versus animal, can assume various meanings and uses even during the same time and in the same place.

chapter 7

The Sociozoologic Scale

In this land of foremost progress—
In this Wisdom's ripest age—
We have placed him, in high honor,
In a monkey's cage!

—Article about an African Bushman exhibited in
the Bronx Zoo, *New York Times,* 1906

ALMOST FORTY YEARS AGO, C. Wright Mills (1959) spoke of the vitality and power of sociological analysis in his classic work, *The Sociological Imagination.* To think this way, according to Mills, is to transcend the personal experiences of everyday life, or what he called "troubles," and locate them in a larger societal or historical context. Look at the falling out and divorce of a married couple. Some would see only their sadness and bitterness. But sociologists also see abstract but nonetheless real cultural forces, such as increased economic pressure on couples or changing sex roles, that explain why divorce rates in contemporary society have gone up. What is so useful, then, about the sociological imagination is that it forces us to look away from the very event or problem that initially catches our interest in order to understand it.

Mills would say that to understand our ambivalence toward animals, we must look beyond it to more general social processes. For example, societies rank everything on a ladder of worth, including people and animals, and systems of social control perpetuate these rankings. Such vertical social orders make inequality of privilege seem "natural," as not everyone or everything will be regarded equally. Those who land at the bottom, because they are in some inferior category, can justifiably be exploited and oppressed. Our ability to rank-order animals—and the inconsistencies that follow—may be a useful form of thinking for systems of social control that seek to justify inconsistent treatment of humans. Once in culture's hands, animals may offer one such social control device. They can become useful vehicles by which humans express their image of society's ladder or serve as a means of enforcing these expectations. Of course, that animal symbols can work this way presumes that members of contemporary societies classify animals not only on biological grounds, but on moral and social ones as well.

A hierarchical model of animals has governed Western thought since Aristotle's notion that nature was ordered on a vertical scale that extended from lifeless things to man. For many centuries, new thinking in Western societies has continued to be influenced by ancient ideas about a "chain of being" (Lovejoy 1936). From the Middle Ages to the eighteenth century, it was thought that God fixed the place of all creatures in nature, with humans having dominion over animals. God was at the pinnacle in this rigid hierarchical chain of being, followed by his representatives and interpreters (church and state), then by the social tiers of feudalism, all of which sat above the kingdom of nonhuman animals, also having its respective ranking from primates to plants. Each living thing was seen as both similar yet different from those immediately above and below it on the scale.

Scholars have thoroughly criticized this way of classifying animals (Birke 1994; Serpell 1986; Thomas 1985), arguing that the chain of being and the theological doctrine behind it wrongly allowed people to consider themselves inherently superior to animals and justified their exploitation of them. Others have criticized more contemporary ways that people classify living beings. Despite Darwin,

Steven Jay Gould (1991) contends, a common misconception is that evolution is a linear progression of life into a final, perfect form with humans arising from apes. This distorted notion of evolution, reminiscent of the earlier chain of being, incorrectly ranks animals on a phylogenetic scale where humans, with their unique traits, are at the pinnacle, while "primitive" organisms or creatures that least resemble humans physically are relegated to the bottom. Gould notes that even when evolution is more accurately portrayed as a branched process, humans are still depicted as superior because those animals at the bottom are considered to be inferior.

Although thinkers like Lynda Birke and Gould are correct to fault the chain of being on logical, moral, and scientific grounds, in some fashion it still lingers on in contemporary thinking. Attempts to eliminate contemporary versions of the chain are likely to fail so long as its critics focus on the scientific nature of classification rather than on the sociological basis for how people in contemporary societies order living beings. The desire continues to put animals on some sort of ladder, not because people are ignorant about science—although they certainly might be—but because some dominant ideas linger over many centuries. The history of ideas has demonstrated that certain notions become so pervasive and central to the thought of a culture that over time people uncritically apply these ideas anew (Douglas 1971).

While phylogenetic systems of classification rank animals on the basis of biological distinctions, sociozoologic systems rank them according to how well they seem to "fit in" and play the roles they are expected to play in society. How well animals seem to know their place and stay in it will determine worth and position on the social ladder. On such a scale, good animals have high moral status because they willingly accept their subordinate place in society, with some able to enjoy their niche while others only dutifully comply with it. They are therefore visibly brought into contact with the human world—of course, on human terms. These animals, by their very behavior, help to define and reinforce the meaning of mainstream society, and are valued for this contribution. However, bad animals have a low moral status because their subordinate place is unclear or because they no longer remain quietly out of sight and distant from people. Since these creatures are perceived as both symbolic and real threats to the social order, they may be killed.

That societies perceive animals as good or bad indicates that social constructions are inherently moral constructions, and in Western societies moral categories are, most typically, dualistic (Douglas 1970). We construct images of good and evil, respectable and disreputable, friend and foe, desirable and undesirable, and countless other morally laden oppositions. Each social construct necessarily implies the existence of its opposite and depends on this opposite for its meaning. Significantly, these oppositions are taken for granted in everyday moral communication and, consequently, exert much force in our lives. They do so by prompting us to take certain actions, even if inconsistent, and then to justify these actions toward animals. Just as the sociozoologic scale justifies inconsistent treatment of animals, the constructs of good and bad animals can similarly justify inconsistent treatment of humans. Dualistic thinking, then, about animals and their place in society is useful as an instrument of social control.

Good Animals

At the top of the sociozoologic scale are humans, although, as we describe below, different groups of humans appear at every rung of the social ladder. Following humans are the best animals—so tame they are almost like humans. Pets seem to love their place in the social order, appearing almost genetically predisposed to be part of the civilized world and eager to learn and follow its ways. Other good animals—those in labs or on farms, for instance—do not seem to desire their given place, but can do little about it. Both kinds of good animals have a valued place in society because they are either affectively useful as companions or instrumentally useful as "tools." Companion animals are regarded as almost human and are treated paternalistically as babies, although they may also be regarded as friends or even coworkers of sorts, and there is a great deal of moral concern for their welfare. Instrumental animals are not regarded as very humanlike but, because they are necessary cogs in the wheels of society, there is interest in their welfare. For both categories, however, there is a fundamental master–servant relationship where the place of the animals is clearly subordinate to that of humans.

Pets

Pet-keeping is a common practice in human societies, and various theorists have tried to explain its cultural origins. Some have argued that early humans domesticated canids because they could play valuable roles in the hunt and could warn of approaching danger. From this perspective, certain wild animals were chosen by humans. However, Stephen Budiansky (1992) contends that these animals also exercised "choice" and sought relationships with humans. As they became "petified," they came to have somewhat less tangible functions in human communities. People turned to the animals living with them as sources of affection and, contrastingly, as beings over whom they could easily exercise dominance (Tuan 1984). In short, pets are animals that came to "love" their keepers. This affectionate domination provides owners with a feeling of supremacy over nature and the power to incorporate animals into the civilized world (Birke 1994). The recent popularity of the term "companion animal" and its implied mutuality is clearly a response to the implied subordination of the conventional pet. Nevertheless, the superior attitude is still prevalent in our modern thinking. Pets, as opposed to companion animals, are regarded by many Americans as subordinates and treated as possessions (Veevers 1985).

Much like animals that submit to authority, groups of people have been regarded as domesticated, quiet, and tame. Accepting (or seeming to accept) their given place in society, they foster a sense of orderliness, subject to the will and social restraints of those in power. According to the dominant group, they need to be taken care of paternalistically like pets, farm animals, or children—so long as they stay in their place. According to Berta Perez (1986, 19), such "petifi-cation" entails confining, domesticating, or diminishing humans in order to make them small. "Making small," in turn, involves con-trolling others so that the others become "creatures of submission," displaying dependency and needing guidance.

Indeed, there are times when the treatment of children and pets is indistinguishable. The child's physical dependency, incomplete so-cialization, and "cute" appearance commonly lead to his or her be-ing dealt with as a kind of pet. This resemblance is especially appar-ent when an adult and child or an owner and pet are both present in a public setting and the child or pet misbehaves. The misbehavior is frequently regarded as the "fault" of the caretaker who is presumed to be competent and in control. Knowing this, adults in the company of children (Cahill 1987) and people with pets (Sanders 1990a) often feel obliged to offer excuses for their charges when they overstep the bounds of public propriety.

Sociologists observe that minority group members who accept their subordinate place in society are often treated like infants or children. This treatment reduces minority members to the status of children—from helpless infants to adolescents who lack moral, in-tellectual, or physical maturity. Depicted as "irresponsible," "impul-sive," "fun-loving," and "immature," minorities are seen as depen-dent on the "more mature" dominant group for their survival or for guidance to accomplish the tasks they are assigned.

The antebellum South provides an appropriate example. The "lit-tle black Sambo" image was used extensively to establish the ideology of a "white man's burden," by which enslaved people would perish without the paternalistic "protection" of whites. To this day, the epi-thet "boy" recalls the infantilization of slavery (Blassingame 1972). Similarly, women before the liberation movement of the 1960s were often called "baby," "girl," "honey," and "sweetie." Their fashions in earlier eras often reflected the clothing worn by infants or teenagers of a previous generation (Lurie 1982).

Old people in America are also infantilized and treated like pets by the media, health-care personnel, or relatives who consider them unable to manage their own lives due to the incapacities of "second childhood." In its most extreme form, infantilization can be found in mass media images of the toothless, hairless, wrinkled, bent, and drooling elder as a "newborn" who is increasingly dependent as he or she approaches death (Arluke and Levin 1990). Like traditional family pets, "senior citizens" may become highly dependent on others who, despite feeling affection for their elders, do not treat them as full-fledged family members.

Tools

Some animals have a clear and valuable place in the social order, although it is not as members of the family. They are useful to humans because they perpetuate various institutions—like that of bench science—or provide products demanded by human society—like those of the farm industry. To become tools, however, their animal nature must be reconstructed as scientific data or food. To accomplish this transformation, animals must be deanthropomorphized, becoming lesser beings or objects that think few thoughts, feel only the most primitive emotions, and experience little pain.

For example, sociologists have documented the process by which animals in laboratories become tools for scientists or students to use in experiments. Such a process acknowledges that the same animal can be thought of as a tool in the context of laboratories while being regarded quite differently from the commonsense viewpoint. The latter, naturalistic animal (Lynch 1988) is found in nature as "wildlife" or in the home as a "pet" and is considered to be capable of experiencing pain and suffering. Even before they arrive in laboratories, the naturalistic identity of animals is stripped away, when breeding companies market lab animals as superobjects—pure and standardized as virtual clones of each other, manufactured and customized to meet science's needs, and submissive and cooperative to make their use in experiments easy (Arluke 1994). Once they are ordered from breeding companies as "supplies," they are systematically incorporated into experiments by assigning them numbers or meaningless names, handled in large batches by giving them corporate rather than individual identities, and defined by laboratory norms as objects rather than as pets (Arluke 1990a). The result is that the animal's body is transformed into data and it is regarded as a different kind of entity from the naturalistic animal. Mary Phillips (1993), for instance, found that scientists rarely provided analgesics to lab animals after surgery. She argues that, like the nineteenth-century savage and drunk that were thought not to need anesthesia because they felt little pain, the contemporary lab animal gets no pain relief. Although scientists will admit that animals are sensitive to pain, it rarely occurs to scientists that lab animals might feel pain because they are defined as scientific data. The view of these animals as existing solely for research overrides concern for their subjective experience.

To use animals as lab materials, definitions of animals and humans have to be mutually exclusive and boundaries between the species will be clearly drawn. That this is so can be seen in the uneasiness of researchers who blur these boundaries and view lab animals as pets (Arluke 1990b). At times, certain minorities and powerless groups of people—retarded children, prisoners, the poor, enlisted soldiers—have been defined as different enough from most humans to be used as lab animals. Like lab animals, they are seen as lower on the social ladder, lesser humans, and therefore eligible for use in experiments that involve greater risk and suffering than those thought appropriate for other humans.

The most infamous American case of transforming humans into tools was the syphilis experiment in Tuskegee, Alabama. For forty years, the U.S. Public Health Service installation there deliberately withheld penicillin from more than four hundred uneducated black sharecroppers and unskilled laborers who suffered from syphilis, in order to study the disease's evolution (Jones 1981). These human "guinea pigs" were not informed that they had syphilis and were duped into cooperating with suggestions that the aspirin and iron tonic given them would cure their "bad blood." That humans could have been used as laboratory animals in an ongoing, long-term study to determine how long it takes syphilis to kill people reflects an astonishing degree of racism as well as bureaucratic failure. Without condoning their actions, we can see that the physicians involved in this experiment echoed attitudes taken for granted among many white middle-class Americans—that the lower classes were composed of "losers," moral failures responsible for their own poverty, sickness, and disease. All of these socially constructed images helped to distance the researchers, enabling them to regard their black subjects as not completely human.

Bad Animals

The place of good animals, whether human or nonhuman, is clear in the social order. They participate as "decent citizens" of a sort by being trustworthy, predictable, and obedient in their given roles. Some animals, however, have a problem with their place in society. They may be freaks that confuse their place, vermin that stray from their place, or demons that reject their place. They are oddities that cause repulsion, unwelcome visitors that provoke fear, or dangerous attackers that rouse horror. In turn, society may ignore, marginalize, segregate, or destroy them.

As is true with good animals, the morally laden symbols of bad animals can serve as useful instruments of human social control—that they are highly flexible symbols makes them all the more useful. Humans who are animalized, whether they are regarded as freaks, vermin, or demons, are labeled capriciously. For example, depictions of rats may be applied to groups that are deemed merely socially undesirable as well as to groups that society views as serious threats to the social order. Thus, the same animal can take on different connotations. In the first group, the rat may be used to invoke a sense of dirtiness or disorder, while in the second it may invoke images of plague-carrying demons that kill human infants. People seem to get the point when an animal construct is used in a certain context. For example, when members of a group are thought to lack either intelligence or morality, perceived as "dumb," or "intellectually inferior," its members might be depicted as nonhuman primates such as apes or chimps, as atavistic beings one step below humans on the phylogenetic scale. If, however, a minority group is seen as intelligent but "evil" or "sinister," its members may be pictured as devil-like or as vicious animals.

Freaks

Some animals do not have a clear place in the social order. Their status is confused and ambiguous because they mix categories that are considered by many people to be pure and sacred. Although there is no urgency to destroy them, their questionable moral status puts them on the margins of society. They are, at best, objects of curiosity, but more likely they are ignored, pitied, scorned, or found repulsive.

Once thought of as evil omens or the products of witches, by the beginning of the nineteenth century these "human curiosities" were seen as part of God's order of beings. Nomenclature rather than cause dominated scientific publications about monsters who were regarded by interested scientists—known as teratologists—as a legitimate subject for study and classification. With Western expansionism in the nineteenth and early twentieth centuries and increased concern about the duty of humans to each other and to other animals, scientific writing turned more to cause than classification. The "hybridity" theory, for one, saw "wild men" and "savages"—whose grunting, pacing, or snarling fed into an image of "animal people"— as the result of crossbreeding between humans and beasts. The "atavistic" theory took a different approach, arguing that these biological confusions were throwbacks to more primitive forms of life. At the root of these popular explanations and attempts at classification was a culture's uncomfortable curiosity and need to account for something seen as fundamentally disordered and wrong.

In the nineteenth and early twentieth centuries, "freaks" that appeared to mix human and animal features were immensely popular in circuses and carnivals (Bogdan 1988). Some aroused interest because of a malformity that reminded people of animals, such as the Giraffe Woman who had long limbs, Jo-Jo the dog-faced boy who had a lot of hair on his face and body, or the Camel Girl whose malformed knees forced her to walk on all fours. Of course, other human–animal freaks were gaffs, thought of as animal-like because they had unusual abilities that mimicked particular animals. Many famous sideshow ingestors were advertised as "human ostriches" because they could swallow objects ranging from nails to watches and contortionists in serpent costumes were labeled "snake men" because they could inch their bodies slowly across the stage.

Today most people commonly respond to such anomalies with fright, disgust, or contempt, because they seem to violate a sense of physical or perhaps even spiritual sacredness or purity. The notion of human–animal mixes makes most people uneasy; they regard it as a contamination of distinctions thought to be holy or sacred. Tabloid newspapers describing human mothers who give birth to babies that are part human, part animal (cf. Herzog and Galvin 1992) pander to the public's fascination with offbeat stories that strike a morally repulsive cord in many people. The text of these stories tells its readers as much, pointing out the mother's horror upon learning of her newborn's mixed nature. No doubt this discomfort accounts for some of the public horror precipitated by the 1984 Baby Fae case, in which an infant received a transplanted baboon's heart at California's Loma Linda Hospital. Similarly, one aspect of the growing public outcry over genetic manipulation is a moral concern over what is seen as the "unnatural" mixing of different animal species, with a potential for producing freaks and monsters.

As an instrument of social control, the construct of freak can be applied to groups of people whose biology is entirely human. The construction of freak, according to Robert Bogdan (1988) and Susan Sontag (1977), has become a metaphor for the dark, or not understood, side of human experience and the marginality that is associated with it. Homeless people, recent immigrants, and various groups of humans are seen as anomalous creatures—not fully human or "like the rest of us" to many Americans. For example, homeless people living in the subway tunnels of New York City are called "mole people," a pejorative term among homeless advocates and an insulting one to some tunnel dwellers, because it conjures up freakish images. Jennifer Toth (1993), for one, notes an informant's objections to the term, "because he feels it is a label that portrays him as an animal, not as a person." Indeed, what makes the image of mole people so striking and disturbing is that one pictures wretched and disgusting subhumans whose abodes might easily be taken for those of burrowing animals. Though Toth humanizes the mole people and dismisses the fantasy that they are animal-like cave dwellers, the freakish and horrible images conjured up by the term "mole people" are exactly the sort of morally laden images that are essential for animal constructs to serve as effective instruments of social control. Although this modern use of freaks places them in the bowels of society, there are still other humans below even them in the sociozoologic scale, because they are seen as greater dangers to the social order.

Vermin

Lower than freaks on this scale are animals that stray from their place, cross human-drawn boundaries, and threaten to contaminate individuals or the environment. Although vermin are not usually a physical threat, people often have feelings of disgust or hatred toward them because they are thought to be literally or symbolically "dirty." They are believed to pollute what is regarded as pure and create disorder out of order. Segregation, avoidance, or destruction are frequent responses to them.

The meaning of mice in a biomedical research facility demonstrates how such vermin are socially constructed and the moral consequences of that construct. Harold Herzog (1988) found that lab mice were not all regarded in the same manner even though they were virtually identical. Some were regarded as "good" animals and others as "bad." Good mice were used in experiments by researchers and graduate students, and presumably lived and died for human benefit. The welfare of these good animals was protected by law, and official committees supervised their use to ensure that they were used and killed humanely. Bad mice were laboratory animals that had escaped into the building and could no longer be used in experiments. As one of Herzog's informants commented: "Once an animal hits the floor, it is a pest." These nuisances lived behind the walls of labs and threatened the sterility of the facility's scientific environment. To prevent cross-contamination of rooms, the researchers moved to exterminate them. Their lowly moral status meant that no one was responsible for overseeing their treatment, so they were often killed quite cruelly. Household mousetraps proved ineffective, and poison was not used because it might contaminate research animals. Finally, sticky traps were used to capture the mice, whose feet stuck to the glue boards; half were found dead on the traps after presumably struggling for some time; the other half were killed by the staff. Herzog points out that death by glue board is not humane, and most committees that oversee animal experimentation would not approve research that glued mice to boards and left them overnight (1988, 473–474).

In certain circumstances, groups of humans may be seen and treated as bad animals because they—like vermin—stray from their culturally determined place. The history of the Jews abounds with examples of their animalization as unwanted pests who come too close for the comfort of other people. During the mass migration of Jews to the United States in the late nineteenth century, anti-Semitism gained momentum. Jews were depicted as subhuman, genetically inferior to Anglo-Saxons, evil, and parasitic. Michael Selzer (1972, 42–43) cites an 1881 publication entitled *The Wolves of New York*, which described Jews as animal-like in their greed. Depicted as "eager for prey and plunder," Jewish businessmen were compared to "ferretlike" creatures with "long clawlike fingers" upon their money, to jackals waiting for the remains of the lion's prey, or to vultures waiting for their meal of carrion. Other publications from this period often characterized the Jew variously as weasel, hedgehog, vampire, bat, or rat. For example, one political cartoon at the turn of the century depicted Jewish entrepreneurs as forming a gigantic octopus (with an enormous nose), whose tentacles enveloped the world.

While Jews and other immigrant groups have been animalized because they were viewed as the human equivalent of vermin, this sentiment was also expressed metaphorically through animals. In the late nineteenth century, for instance, sparrows were hunted down with a vengeance even though they were not carrying disease, threatening crops, providing food, or serving as sport trophies. According to Gary Fine and Lazaros Christoforides (1991), the sparrows served as metaphor for immigrants coming into this country. At that time, America was rife with controversy over new immigrants; to some Americans, they were inferior human beings—filthy, immoral, and dangerous—who should not be allowed onto our shores. Others disagreed, and a vigorous public debate ensued. Simultaneously, an equally heated—and symbolically related—debate took place among ornithologists, some of whom maintained that sparrows were a menace to the American ecosystem and should, therefore, be systematically exterminated. Although there was no scientific support for this position, those who called for elimination of sparrows employed the same imagery used by nativists of the day. The birds were foreign, immoral; they competed unfairly with other birds and should be extirpated from the American bird community. The sparrow controversy, then, mirrored debates over immigration. For nativists, both sparrows and immigrants were dirty, bad, and morally suspect and, therefore, "out of place" in the clean and morally upright culture of America.

Demons

Below vermin on the sociozoologic scale are the worst animals—commonly portrayed in popular culture as fiends, predators, or man-eaters—that contest the established social order itself. Vermin may refuse to stay in their lowly place, but demons mount a more serious and "evil" challenge to the way things "ought to be" by trying to reverse the fundamental master–servant relationship present in the traditional phylogenetic order. These animals do not fear humans, humans fear them. These animals hunt humans, humans do not hunt them. These animals have power over humans, humans do not have power over them. The typical response to demons is to kill them before they disempower or kill humans.

One well-known example of demons reversing the master–servant relationship can be seen in the portrayal of werewolves in American film. On their surface, these films, from Lon Chaney, Jr, in the 1940 *Wolf Man* to John Landis' 1981 *American Werewolf in London,* are about the transformation of humans into murderous, evil beasts, but at a deeper level they are about the transformation of traditional relationships between the species. In the most recent werewolf film, Mike Nichols' 1994 *Wolf,* Jack Nicholson acquires superhuman powers after being bitten by a wolf. He discovers a new strength, cunning, and stamina. Even his senses become far sharper than those of normal humans; he can smell tequila on a colleague's breath from the other side of the hallway and hear low voices a floor away. Nicholson's new powers allow him to pursue terrified human game as he takes revenge on a colleague who has usurped his job and his wife. After all attempts to kill Nicholson fail, the wolfman and those he has bitten make a final and complete transformation into wolves.

Groups of humans may be demonized if they are seen as "uppity" and a threat to majority-group domination and the established social ladder, particularly members of minority or out-groups, when they have challenged the status quo. Once people are depicted as demons, even the most brutal treatment of them may seem appropriate because they are regarded as more dangerous than vermin; the latter, after all, merely contaminate culture, they do not challenge its fundamental social makeup.

Upon their arrival in the New World, blacks were regarded as "devils incarnate" by white settlers who tried desperately to rationalize the brutality of the slave regime. The submissive "Sambo" image appeared only after the slave system had been institutionalized for some time and a certain level of compliance had been assured.

The demonization of black Americans occurred again during Reconstruction, as white groups felt their social and economic status directly threatened by the newly emancipated slaves. For example, in 1867, during the controversy over blacks' voting rights, a pamphlet, "The Negro: What Is His Ethnological Status?" argued that blacks were not descendants of Adam and Eve but had entered Noah's ark with the beasts. The author declared, "You can not elevate a beast to the level of a son of God—a son of Adam and Eve—but you may depress the sons of Adam and Eve, with their impress of the Almighty, down to the level of a beast" (quoted in Craige 1992, 122). From the viewpoint of many white people, what was really threatened was their larger "culture"—changing rules would change relationships that took centuries to develop.

By the turn of the century, poor whites were bombarded with propaganda concerning their duty to maintain the purity of the white race. Racist literature of the day argued that blacks were a subhuman species whose members should be forced out of the United States (Frazier 1949; Woodward 1966). For example, in a publication of 1900 entitled "The Negro a Beast," the author claimed that blacks were "simply beasts without souls." According to E. Franklin Frazier (1962), "In every representation of the Negro, he was pictured as a gorilla dressed up like a man. . . . In the newspapers the Negro was described as burly or ape-like and even Negroes who look like whites were represented in cartoons as black with gorilla features. All this fitted into the stereotype which represented the Negro as subhuman or a beast, without any human qualities." During this campaign to prove that blacks were subhuman, they were also portrayed as "lower animals" devoid of morals and higher emotions. Frazier also notes that a 1910 Columbia University doctoral dissertation stated that blacks were "as destitute of morals as any of the lower animals" and a 1915 book by an Army surgeon that "many animals below man manifest a far greater amount of real affection in their love-making" (pp. 144–45).

Women have been demonized for similar reasons. In the 1920s, when organized groups of women mounted political protest directed toward obtaining the right to vote, they commonly were referred to as "flappers" (i.e., birds leaving the nest). When "Rosie the Riveter" was assuming traditionally masculine jobs in World War II factories, women were sometimes called "alligators." In the 1960s and 1970s, feminist leaders were often accused of wanting to invert the established social order (Craige 1992). It was thought that if feminists did not accept men as superior to women, then they must believe that women were superior to men. It was also argued that any increase in the rights, prestige, or power of women meant a decrease in those attributes for men. Change in rank-order means redistribution of resources, and that is tantamount to revolution. In 1971, the FBI started a file on the women's movement. During this period, the "little girl" image of women was overshadowed by the more ominous stereotypes of animals and demons. In everyday conversation, where women typically had been referred to in infantile terms, they were now also addressed as pets or animals, as in "bunny," "pussy," "chick," "bird," and "fox." Members of the liberation movement, but especially their leaders, were called "Amazons" and "bitch-goddesses." The most extreme demonization appeared in sadomasochistic pornography in which women were shown as slavelike animals and sexual objects to be used and tortured.

While it may be years before it becomes clear in retrospect who our contemporary bad animals are, data strongly suggest that certain groups are even now being pictured this way. And once again, animals may be useful symbols to accomplish this labeling. Take the case of pit bulls. Hearne (1991) chronicles the story of the pit bull Bandit who, because of his alleged "viciousness" was ordered to be destroyed by the State of Connecticut. Although not actually a pit bull, Bandit was described in court and by the media just as demonically as most Americans would describe the breed. People insisted that Bandit's "uncontrollability" or "unpredictability" meant that he eventually would turn on someone without provocation or warning, and his "meanness" was seen as residing in his genes. Although Hearne debunks the case against Bandit and pit bulls in general, the image of these dogs as killers continues to linger.

To a large segment of the public, pit bulls are more than dangerous killers; they are demons that eat humans. Hearne describes the
investigation of a "monster" pit bull in New York City that was said
not only to have killed a victim but to have eaten him, too. Autopsy
reports, however, discredited this story. The victim's body had razor
cuts rather than dog-bite wounds, suggesting that a murderer cut up
the body and fed it to the dog. Nor is New York the only city where
a pit bull has been blamed for a death caused by a human.

What is behind this fear and what does it tell us about the relationships of humans to other humans as well as to animals? From the
mid- to late 1980s, several American cities reported an epidemic of
pit bull bites, many of which allegedly were fatal. Serious attacks by
these dogs seemed to increase sharply, for no discernible reason. Any
episode involving a pit bull became cause for widespread alarm,
being seen as part of a larger pattern, both new and exclusive to this
one breed of dog. All of a sudden the American media had its latest
number-one enemy. The headline of a 1987 article in *U.S. News and
World Report* proclaimed that pit bulls were "The Most Dangerous
Dog in America." "America's baddest dog," claimed the author, was
in a separate league from shepherds, Dobermans, and rottweilers,
because they cannot "chomp through a chain-link fence" like pit
bulls. Cities passed ordinances that restricted or banned pit bulls, and
the media kept the hysteria going by reporting every pit bull attack
while ignoring those of other breeds. One pit bull, as evidence of the
uproar, was firebombed while it was playing in its own enclosure;
and some of this public hysteria was also directed at pit bull owners.

Although pit bulls can become extremely dangerous, claim veterinary experts, statistical data do not show that these dogs are over-
represented among biting animals (Rowan 1986). The evidence suggests that pit bull bites were just as common long before the rash of
newspaper stories; so were biting incidents involving lots of Saint
Bernards, huskies, malamutes, and Great Danes. And, according to
Hearne, the statistics themselves were extremely unreliable—many
were collected secondhand, the definition of a dog bite was ambiguous, and the breed of the attacking dog was itself often not reported.

Hearne argues that pit bulls became a metaphor for something larger and scarier to many people who displaced their fear onto these dogs. Reports of attacks by these dogs were invariably accompanied by value-laden descriptions of their owners that were guaranteed to threaten mainstream America. More academically restrained criticisms of these owners noted, with anecdotal evidence only, that ownership of pit bulls was macho; presumably, the meaner the dog, the meaner the human (Rowan 1986). Capitalizing on class fears, pit bull reports by the media and even some humane organizations were peppered with references to poor urban blacks and Hispanics who kept their dogs in dope dens and fed them raw meat to make them as mean as possible, or less often, to heavily tattooed white thugs with shaved heads who starved their heavily chained dogs to increase their ferociousness. "Decent citizens" were not at the root of the pit bull problem, because they were responsible owners, according to the press.

People's fear was certainly stirred up, but it may have been as much or more their fear of a perceived dangerous class of evil humans than a breed of dogs. Was it dogs or humans whose behavior needed to become "more appropriate and docile"? Why else did sensational media stories about pit bulls suddenly vanish by the late 1980s? Certainly, efforts to curtail their attacks or change their breeding could not have had such an immediate effect. Having a short half-life in the media, the pit bull crisis faded as quickly as it had started. These dogs were a convenient hook on which to hang our growing sense of vulnerability to crime and our fear for personal safety—not from dogs—but from other humans.

Members of the underclass, then, may be becoming our modern demons, at least to mainstream America. Feeling threatened by them on the streets and imprisoned at home, many Americans fear for their personal safety and experience angst over losing control over the social fabric. They describe these humans as demonic, antisocial creatures who live in a culture of sociopathy—outside the pale of the civilized world. Of course, this view of the underclass is distorted, but that is irrelevant. It is the construction of its members as a growing and encroaching "menace" to America that is sociologically important. Indeed, according to sociologist Jack Levin (1994), this fear and hatred has become so common and intense among America's white middle class that it rates a special term—"afrophobia"—when it is targeted at members of the black underclass who are seen as dangerous thugs, murderers, and rapists.

Examining the hierarchical structure of meaning that humans devise to situate and comprehend themselves and other beings returns us to the central issue of this volume. By understanding how we define and relate to criminals we can come closer to understanding ourselves. Whether pet or demon, tool or vermin, the sociozoologic scale is a type of story that humans—with the help of animals—tell themselves and each other about the meaning of "place" in modern societies. As stories often do, they explain and rationalize certain relationships that are expected of people—where they belong in or out of society and how they are expected to behave. Those who believe and even share a particular story probably do not see the inconsistency of their own behavior toward other groups. Quite the contrary, they may feel that their actions—even if seen by others as hypocritical—are morally justified. That social constructions of animals are highly flexible and rich symbols—as pointed out years ago by anthropologists who knew that animals are "good to think"—is no doubt why animals are such useful instruments through which humans can express their conflicted feelings toward fellow humans.

conclusion

Paradox and Change

AMBIVALENCE HAS ALWAYS CHARACTERIZED human treatment of animals, and the modern age is certainly no exception. Indeed, our society is shot through with conflicts running across all groups and circumstances. It is true, of course, that more people than ever before suffer conflicts over their use of animals. More people than ever before feel that it matters what we do to animals. And more people than ever before are committed to an ideal of "humaneness" that sees suffering as wrong. Yet, alongside these recent concerns are "inherited practices" that uphold this ambivalence (Midgley 1989, 85) and make it normal. These practices make it possible, we argue, for many people to live with contradictions without being troubled by or even aware of them.

In Chapter 3 we found that everyday knowledge of animals is inherently contradictory, as is much common sense in general. While scholars and critics often call attention to these contradictions as serious problems, apparently for laypersons they are not. Rather than trying to eliminate these inconsistencies, the latter group simply works around them. Steve Baker (1993) sees this in our popular imagination as reflected in the media. Here, he claims, commonsense knowledge easily accommodates contradictions because its rhetorical conventions disregard the boundaries between what is real, representational, or symbolic. This confusion is not troublesome for ordinary persons because commonsense knowledge is not constrained to be consistent. So, too, outside the media. We saw how the use of commonsense knowledge by animal owners and trainers allowed them to shift, when necessary, between two very different conceptions of dogs.

As we noted in Chapter 4, people working in an animal shelter had to rely on a different kind of inherited practice. They needed to acquire a second self—an institutional one in addition to the everyday self—in order to euthanize dogs and cats. Were shelter workers seriously conflicted or troubled because they euthanized animals? Again, as we have seen with other inconsistencies, most people, most of the time, were not. Of course, there are areas of consistency or central tendencies within the human self (Serpe 1987), and people generally do prefer to have a stable, consistent image of who they are (Elliott 1986). However, K. J. Gergen (1972, 1978) asserts that too much attention is paid to such central tendencies and too little attention to the complexities of the self. Most people today do not develop an entirely coherent sense of self and this, in fact, is how they learn to live and survive in the contemporary world. Those few who do develop one may even suffer emotionally for it.

Modern life in Western societies is also marked by a plurality of meanings. These systems of meanings are another inherited practice that makes possible the inconsistent treatment of animals. Were the technicians in Chapter 5 aware of the existence of alternative meanings of animals in other labs? The few who worked in more than one primate lab had this awareness. Most did not and assumed, as we would expect, that the way animals were regarded at their lab held true elsewhere. Some, when questioned more closely, vaguely speculated that animals might be regarded differently in other centers. However, technicians usually were surprised when they discovered the extent of these differences. Their response to this information was one of incredulity but not of anguish. Forced to stop and think about the fragmentation of their taken-for-granted reality, for a few seconds they became conscious of themselves and the relativity of their worldview (Berger 1979).

Boundary work is yet another inherited practice that enables people to live with inconsistency. As we demonstrated in Chapter 6, it expedited a most unsavory contradiction in Nazi Germany where animals were sometimes better regarded than humans. Did Germans experience their paradoxical treatment of humans and animals as a twisted and grotesque logic? We would say they did not, because it was normative for Nazi Germans to behave cruelly and inhumanely toward polluted "lower" beings and affectionately and humanely toward morally elevated animals. Boundary blurring was part of the moral and intellectual context of Nazi Germany. Rather than its being seen as an inconsistency, in Nazi Germany it could exist as a consistency, given the consanguinity of certain "higher" humans and animals and the lack of consanguinity of certain humans and other humans.

It would be wrong to think of this period in Germany as a fluke of history. In Chapter 7 it should be evident that different groups of people, in other places and at other times, also have drawn or blurred species boundaries to justify the inconsistent treatment of humans themselves. How conflicted were those people who saw immigrants as dirty sparrows, women as bitches, blacks as lab animals, or old people as pets? Not at all. Nowhere was this point made clearer than in Gunnar Myrdal's *An American Dilemma* (1944), which showed how Americans could maintain racist attitudes toward Americans of African descent while professing to believe in equality. Did this paradox between racism and democratic ideals become invisible because of the historical and cultural mechanisms that existed to justify it? Sociologically, the answer is yes—to the extent that this paradox was built into the culture in the same way that apple pie and motherhood are passed on to future generations as part of the American way of life. While inconsistency does occasionally come into an individual's awareness as a glaring problem calling for correction, most of the time, most people live comfortably with contradictions as a natural and normal part of everyday life.

Reaching this conclusion may disturb some readers who think we have been too dispassionate in our analysis, describing rather than judging. As ethnographers, we have chosen to study the lives, professions, and social worlds of people to understand rather than criticize, explain rather than preach. Yet it is true that there are potential "costs" involved when people learn to live with their contradictions (Serpell 1995). For example, it may lead to the social isolation of groups of people who may find it easier to associate only with others "in the same boat" who will not point out these contradictions. There is also the potential cost to both individuals and society of allowing, or even condoning, the existence of such contradictions in public attitudes because this dulls our moral sensitivities. As James Nelson (1989, 88) tells us, such acceptance makes contradictions go on not in "the spirit of fear and trembling appropriate to the difficult balancing of significant values but rather in a routinized fashion." Thus, it could be argued that it is appropriate and healthy to challenge these sorts of inconsistencies, even if people find the challenges uncomfortable or disconcerting.

For those who decry this routinization, we believe there is reason for some optimism. In our own research findings, there are seeds of moral progress if that is defined as awareness of contradiction. For instance, although shelter workers learned to behave in ways that were sometimes contrary to their original attitudes, they did so because it was customary and protective. This does not mean that it was a comfortable state for everyone or that their work roles completely merged with their private selves. When their basic culture leaked through their institutional veneer, all shelter workers experienced conflict. Situations in both primate labs forced people to become aware of inconsistencies. Although the sites had opposing perspectives toward animals, there were small pockets of resistance to the predominant view of primates espoused at each lab. Occasionally, these differences erupted into clashes over the appropriate treatment of animals, thrusting contradiction into everyone's awareness.

For those who seek a redressing of society's inconsistencies, there may also be reason for optimism. As we discovered in Chapter 1, the meanings of animals are not fixed because they are social constructions. How we think about animals, as well as ourselves, is bound to change as society itself changes. Some would find, for example, that the sociozoologic scale as we have known it is already crumbling, giving way to a less hierarchical view of human and animal kind. Betty Jean Craige (1992), for one, contends that in recent years there has been a radical transformation of Western culture to a more inclusive, less hierarchical, and less oppressive social order. Such change offers hope that our inconsistent treatment of animals may also be resolved.

references

Adams, Carol. 1990. *The Sexual Politics of Meat: A Feminist–Vegetarian Critical Theory.* New York: Continuum.

Agar, Michael. 1980. *The Professional Stranger.* New York: Academic Press.

Albert, Alexis, and Kris Bulcroft. 1987. "Pets and Urban Life." *Anthrozoös* 1:9–23.

AMA. 1933. "New Regulations Concerning Vivisection." *Journal of the American Medical Association* 102:1087.

Arluke, Arnold. 1990a. "Moral Elevation in Medical Research." In Gary Albrecht, ed., *Advances in Medical Sociology,* 189–204. Greenwich, Conn.: JAI Press.

———. 1990b. "Uneasiness Among Laboratory Technicians." *Lab Animal* 19(4):20–39.

———. 1991. "Going Into the Closet with Science: Information Control Among Animal Experimenters." *Journal of Contemporary Ethnography* 20:306–330.

———. 1994. "'We Build a Better Beagle': Fantastic Creatures in Lab Animal Ads." *Qualitative Sociology* 17:143–158.

Arluke, Arnold, and Frederic Hafferty. 1996. "From Apprehension to Fascination with 'Dog Lab': The Use of Absolutions by Medical Students." *Journal of Contemporary Ethnography* 25:191–209.

Arluke, Arnold, and Jack Levin. 1990. "Second Childhood: Old Age in Popular Culture." In William Feigelman, ed., *Readings on Social Problems,* 261–265. New York: Holt.

Baer, Ted. 1989. *Communicating with Your Dog.* Hauppauge, N.Y.: Barrons.

Baker, Steve. 1993. *Picturing the Beast: Animals, Identity, and Representation.* Manchester, England: University of Manchester Press.

Barnard, Neal. 1990. "The Nazi Experiments." *The Animal's Agenda,* April, 8–9.

Baümler-Schleinkofer, A. 1990. "Biologie unter dem Hakenkreuz: Biologie und Schule im Dritten Reich." *Universitas* 547:54–55.

Bayles, William. 1940. *Caesars in Goosestep.* New York: Harper Bros.

Beck, Alan, and Aaron Katcher. 1983. *Between Pets and People*. New York: Putnam.

Becker, Ernest. 1981. "From Animal to Human Reactivity." In Gregory Stone and Harvey Farberman, eds., *Social Psychology Through Symbolic Interaction*, 91–95. 2d ed. New York: Wiley.

Becker, Howard. 1967. "Whose Side Are We On?" *Social Problems* 14: 239–247.

Becker, Howard and Blanche Geer. 1957. "Participant Observation and Interviewing: A Comparison." *Human Organization* 16:28–32.

———. 1960. "Participant Observation: The Analysis of Qualitative Field Data." In R. N. Adams and J. J. Preiss, eds., *Human Organization Research*, 267–289. Homewood, Ill. Dorsey Press.

Beer, Colin. 1991. "From Folk Psychology to Cognitive Ethology." In Carolyn Ristau, ed., *Cognitive Ethology: The Minds of Other Animals, 19–33*. Hillsdale, N.J.: Lawrence Erlbaum.

Bekoff, Marc. 1994. "Cognitive Ethology and the Treatment of Non-Human Animals: How Matters of Mind Inform Matters of Welfare." *Animal Welfare* 3:75–96.

Belk, Russell. 1988. "Possessions and the Extended Self." *Journal of Consumer Research* 15:139–168.

Bendersky, Joseph. 1985. *History of Nazi Germany*. Chicago: Nelson-Hall.

Berger, Peter. 1979. *The Heretical Imperative*. Garden City, N.Y.: Anchor Press.

Berger, Peter, and Thomas Luckmann. 1966. *The Social Construction of Reality*. New York: Doubleday.

Bird, Frederick, Frances Westley, and James Waters. 1989. "The Uses of Moral Talk: Why Do Managers Talk Ethics?" *Journal of Business Ethics* 8:75–89.

Birke, Lynda. 1994. *Feminism, Animals, and Science*. Buckingham, England: Open University Press.

Blake, Henry. 1975. *Talking with Horses: A Study of Communication Between Man and Horse*. London: Souvenir Press.

Blassingame, John. 1972. *The Slave Community*. New York: Oxford University Press.

Bloor, Michael. 1983. "Notes on Member Validation." In Robert Emerson, ed., *Contemporary Field Research*, 156–172. Boston: Little, Brown.

Bogdan, Robert. 1988. *Freak Show*. Chicago: University of Chicago Press.

Bogdan, Robert, and Steven Taylor. 1975. *Introduction to Qualitative Research Methods: A Phenomenological Approach to Social Sciences*. New York: Wiley.

———. 1989. "Relationships with Severely Disabled People: The Social Construction of Humanness." *Social Problems* 36:135–148.

Bookbinder, Paul. 1989. Personal Communication.

————. 1993. "'Nazi Animal Protection': A Response." *Anthrozoös* 6:75–78.

Bosk, Charles. 1985. "The Fieldworker as Watcher and Witness," *Hastings Center Report,* June 10–13.

Brady, Robert. 1969. *The Spirit and Structure of German Fascism.* New York: Howard Fertig.

Bramwell, Anna. 1989. *Ecology in the Twentieth Century: A History.* New Haven: Yale University Press.

Brandenburg, Jim. 1988. *White Wolf: Living with an Arctic Legend.* Minocqua, Wisc.: Northword.

Brazelton, T. Berry. 1984. "Four Stages in the Development of Mother-Infant Interaction." In Noboru Kobayashi and T. B. Brazelton, eds., *The Growing Child in Family and Society,* 19–34. Tokyo: University of Tokyo Press.

Bretschneider, Hubert. 1962. *Der Streit um die Vivisektion im 19. Jahrhundert.* Stuttgart: Gustav Fisher.

Bright, Michael. 1990. *Barks, Roars, and Siren Songs.* New York: Carol.

Bromberg, Norbert, and Verna Small. 1983. *Hitler's Psychopathology.* New York: International Universities Press.

Bruyn, Severyn. 1966. *The Human Perspective in Sociology: The Methodology of Participant Observation.* Englewood Cliffs, N.J.: Prentice Hall.

Bryant, Clifton. 1979. "The Zoological Connection: Animal Related Human Behavior." *Social Forces* 58:399–421.

————. 1993. "The Nazi Posture Toward Animals." *Anthrozoös* 9:78–81.

Bryant, Clifton, and Donald Shoemaker. 1988. "Dead Zoo Chic: Some Conceptual Notes on Taxidermy in American Social Life." *Free Inquiry in Creative Sociology* 16:195–202.

Buber, Martin. 1958. *I and Thou.* Translated by Ronald Smith. 2d ed. New York: Scribner's.

Buchanan, Allen, and Dan Brock. 1989. *Deciding for Others: The Ethics of Surrogate Decision Making.* New York: Cambridge University Press.

Budiansky, Stephen. 1992. *The Covenant of the Wild: Why Animals Chose Domestication.* New York: Morrow.

Bulcroft, Kris, George Helling, and Alexa Albert. 1986. "Pets as Intimate Others." Paper presented at Midwest Sociological Society meeting, May.

Burgess, Robert. 1984. "Autobiographical Accounts and Research Experience." In Robert Burgess, ed., *The Research Process in Educational Settings: Ten Case Studies,* 251–270. London: Falmer Press.

Burghardt, Gordon. 1985. "Animal Awareness: Current Perceptions and Historical Perspective." *American Psychologist* 40:905–919.

———. 1991. "Cognitive Ethology and Critical Anthropomorphism: A Snake with Two Heads and Hog-Nosed Snakes That Play Dead." In Carolyn Ristau, ed., *Cognitive Ethology: The Minds of Other Animals*, 53–90. Hillsdale, N.J.: Lawrence Erlbaum.

Cahill, Spencer. 1987. "Children and Civility: Ceremonial Deviance and the Acquisition of Ritual Competence." *Social Psychology Quarterly* 50:312–321.

———. 1990. "Childhood and Public Life: Reaffirming Biographical Divisions." *Social Problems* 37:390–402.

Cain, Ann. 1983. "A Study of Pets in the Family System." In Aaron Katcher and Alan Beck, eds., *New Perspectives on Our Lives with Companion Animals*, 72–81. Philadelphia: University of Pennsylvania Press.

———. 1985. "Pets as Family Members." In Marvin Sussman, ed., *Pets and the Family,* 5–10. New York: Haworth.

Cantwell, Monica. 1993. "Dogs as Racing Machines." Paper presented at the annual meeting of the American Sociological Association, Miami. August.

Carmack, Betty. 1985. "The Effects on Family Members and Functioning After the Death of a Pet." In Marvin Sussman, ed., *Pets and the Family,* 149–161. New York: Haworth.

Chaucer, Geoffrey. 1969. *Complete Works.* Edited by Walter Skeat. Oxford: Oxford University Press.

Cheney, Dorothy, and Robert Seyfarth. 1990. *How Monkeys See the World.* Chicago: University of Chicago Press.

———. 1991. "Truth and Deception in Animal Communication." In Carolyn Ristau, ed., *Cognitive Ethology: The Minds of Other Animals*, 127–151. Hillsdale, N.J.: Lawrence Erlbaum.

Chomsky, Noam. 1980. *Rules and Representations.* New York: Columbia University Press.

Clark, Stephen. 1984. *The Nature of the Beast.* New York: Oxford University Press.

Coe, Rodney M., and Christopher Prendergast. 1985. "The Formation of Coalitions: Interactive Strategies in Triads." *Sociology of Health and Illness* 7:236–247.

Cohen, Joseph. 1989. "About Steaks Liking to Be Eaten: The Conflicting Views of Symbolic Interactionists and Talcott Parsons Concerning the Nature of Relations Between Persons and Non-Human Objects." *Symbolic Interaction* 12:191–214.

Comaroff, John, and Jean Comaroff. 1992. *Ethnography and the Historical Imagination*. Boulder, Colo.: Westview.

Cook, Judith, and Mary Fonow. 1986. "Knowledge and Women's Interests: Issues of Epistemology and Methodology in Feminist Sociological Research." *Sociological Inquiry* 56:2–29.

Cooke, David. 1988. "Animal Disposal: Fact and Fiction." In William Kay et al., eds., *Euthanasia of the Companion Animal*, 224–234. Philadelphia: Charles Press.

Cooley, Charles H. [1902] 1960. *Human Nature and the Social Order*. New York: Schocken.

———. 1927. *Life and the Student*. New York: Knopf.

Coren, Stanley. 1994. *The Intelligence of Dogs*. New York: Free Press.

Cowles, Kathleen. 1985. "The Death of a Pet: Human Responses to the Breaking of the Bond." In Marvin Sussman, ed., *Pets and the Family*, 135–148. New York: Haworth.

Craige, Betty Jean. 1992. *Laying the Ladder Down*. Amherst: University of Massachusetts Press.

Crist, Eileen, and Michael Lynch. 1990. "The Analyzability of Human–Animal Interaction: The Case of Dog Training." Paper presented at the International Sociological Association meeting, Madrid. July.

Cullen, David. "Dog's Killing Stirs Outrage." *Boston Globe*, April 9, 1992, 1, 24.

Darwin, Charles. 1871. *The Descent of Man and Selection in Relation to Sex*. London: John Murray.

Denzin, Norman. 1977. *Childhood Socialization*. San Francisco: Jossey-Bass.

———. 1989. *Interpretive Interactionism*. Newbury Park, Calif.: Sage Publications.

Deuel, Wallace. 1942. *People Under Hitler*. New York: Harcourt Brace.

Deutscher, Irwin. 1973. *What We Say/What We Do: Sentiments and Acts*. Glenview, Ill.: Scott, Foresman.

Diamond, Irene, and Gloria Orenstein, eds. 1990. *Reweaving the World: The Emergence of Ecofeminism*. San Francisco: Sierra Club.

Dicks, Henry. 1972. *Licensed Mass Murder: A Socio-Psychological Study of Some SS Killers*. New York: Basic Books.

di Leonardo, Micaela, ed. 1991. *Gender at the Crossroads: Feminist Anthropology in the Postmodern Era*. Berkeley: University of California Press.

Donnelly, Peter. 1994. "Take My Word for It: Trust in Birding and Mountaineering." *Qualitative Sociology* 17:215–241.

Donovan, Josephine. 1990. "Animal Rights and Feminist Theory." *Signs* 15: 350–375.

Douglas, Jack, ed. 1970. *Deviance and Respectability: The Social Construction of Moral Meanings*. New York: Basic Books.

————. 1971. *American Social Order: Social Rules in a Pluralistic Society*. New York: Free Press.

————. 1976. *Investigative Social Research: Individual and Team Field Research*. Beverly Hills, Calif.: Sage Publications.

Douglas, Mary. 1966. *Purity and Danger: An Analysis of Concepts of Pollution and Taboo*. London: Routledge and Kegan Paul.

Dowd, James J. 1991. "Social Psychology in a Postmodern Age: A Discipline Without a Subject." *American Sociologist* 22:188–209.

Dupre, John. 1990. "The Mental Lives of Nonhuman Animals." In Marc Bekoff and Dale Jamieson, eds., *Interpretation and Explanation in the Study of Animal Behavior*, 1:428–448. Boulder, Colo.: Westview.

Eddy, Timothy, Gordon Gallup, Jr., and Daniel Povinelli. 1993. "Attribution of Cognitive States to Animals: Anthropomorphism in Comparative Perspective." *Journal of Social Issues* 49:87–101.

Edelman, Murray. 1981. "The Political Language of the Helping Professions." In Oscar Grusky and Melvin Pollner, eds., *The Sociology of Mental Illness*, 329–334. New York: Holt, Rinehart, and Winston.

Elliott, Gregory. 1986. "Self-Esteem and Self-Consistency: A Theoretical and Empirical Link Between Two Primary Motivations." *Social Psychology Quarterly* 49:207–218.

Ellis, Carolyn. 1991. "Sociological Introspection and Emotional Experience." *Symbolic Interaction* 14:23–50.

Ellis, Carolyn, and Michael Flaherty, eds. 1992. *Investigating Subjectivity: Research on Lived Experience*. Newbury Park, Calif.: Sage Publications.

Ellis, Donald. 1991. "Post-Structuralism and Language: Non-Sense." *Communication Monographs* 58:213–223.

Emerson, Robert. 1983. *Contemporary Field Research*. Boston: Little, Brown.

Evans-Pritchard, E. E. 1956. *Nuer Religion*. Oxford: Oxford University Press.

Fest, Joachim. 1970. *The Face of the Third Reich*. New York: Pantheon.

————. 1975. *Hitler*. New York: Vintage.

Fine, Gary, and Lazaros Christoforides. 1991. "Dirty Birds, Filthy Immigrants, and the English Sparrow War: Metaphorical Linkage in Constructing Social Problems." *Symbolic Interaction* 14:375–393.

Fisher, John. 1991. "Disambiguating Anthropomorphism: An Interdisciplinary

Review." In P.P.G. Bateson and Peter Klopfer, eds., *Perspectives on Ethology* 9:49–85. New York: Plenum.

Fogle, Bruce. 1990. *The Dog's Mind: Understanding Your Dog's Behavior.* New York: Howell.

Fontana, Andrea, and Ronald Smith. 1989. "Alzheimer's Disease Victims: The 'Unbecoming' of Self and the Normalization of Competence." *Sociological Perspectives* 32:35–46.

Forthman, Debra, Suzanne Elder, Roger Bakeman, Timothy Kurkowski, Constance Noble, and Samuel Winslow. 1992. "Effects of Feeding Enrichment on Behavior of Three Species of Captive Bears." *Zoo Biology* 11:187–195.

Fossey, Dian. 1983. *Gorillas in the Mist.* Boston: Houghton Mifflin.

Fox, Michael. 1990. *Inhumane Society.* New York: St. Martin's.

Frazier, E. Franklin. 1949. *The Negro in the United States.* New York: Macmillan.

———. 1962. *Black Bourgeoisie.* New York: Macmillan.

Gailey, Christine. 1990. Personal communication.

Gal, Susan. 1991. "Between Speech and Silence: The Problematics of Research on Language and Gender." In Micaela di Leonardo, ed., *Gender at the Crossroads: Feminist Anthropology in the Postmodern Era,* 175–203. Berkeley: University of California Press.

Galliher, John. 1980. "Social Scientists' Ethical Responsibilities to Superordinates: Looking Upward Meekly." *Social Problems* 27:298–308.

Gallup, George. 1982. "Self-Awareness and the Emergence of Mind in Primates." *American Journal of Primatology* 2:237–248.

Gasman, Daniel. 1971. *The Scientific Origins of National Socialism: Social Darwinism in Ernst Haeckel and the German Monist League.* New York: American Elsevier.

Geer, Blanche, Jack Haas, Charles Vi Vona, Stephen Miller, Clyde Woods, and Howard Becker. 1968. "Learning the Ropes: Situational Learning in Four Occupational Training Programs." In Irwin Deutscher and Elizabeth Thompson, eds., *Among the People: Encounters with the Poor,* 209–233. New York: Basic Books.

Geertz, Clifford. 1972. "Deep Play: Notes on the Balinese Cockfight." *Daedalus* 101:1–27.

———. 1973. *The Interpretation of Cultures.* New York: Basic Books.

———. 1974. "'From the Native's Point of View': On the Nature of Anthropological Understanding." *Bulletin of the American Academy of Arts and Sciences* 28:27–45.

George, Jean. 1985. *How to Talk to Your Animals.* New York: Harcourt Brace Jovanovich.

Georges, Robert, and Michael Jones. 1980. *People Studying People.* Berkeley: University of California Press.

Gergen, K. J. 1972. "Multiple Identity." *Psychology Today* 5:31–35, 64–66.

———. 1978. "Toward Generative Theory." *Journal of Personality and Social Psychology* 36:1344–1360.

Giese, C., and D. Kahler. 1944. *Das Deutsche Tierschutzrecht: Bestimmungen Zum Schutze der Tiere.* Berlin: Dunker and Humbolt.

Giesler, A. 1938. *Biotechik.* Leipzig: Quelle and Meher.

Gittleman, Sol. 1993. "Comments on Arluke/Sax Article." *Anthrozoös* 6:81–82.

Glaser, Barney, and Anselm Strauss. 1967. *The Discovery of Grounded Theory.* Chicago: Aldine.

Glaser, Hermann. 1978. *The Cultural Roots of National Socialism.* Translated by Ernest Menze. Austin: University of Texas Press.

Goebbels, Joseph. 1948. *The Goebbels Diaries, 1942–1943.* Edited by Louis Lochner. Westport, Conn.: Greenwood.

———. 1983. *The Goebbels Diaries, 1939–1941.* Translated and edited by Fred Taylor. New York: Putnam.

Goffman, Erving. 1971. *Relations in Public.* New York: Basic Books.

Goodall, Jane. 1986. *The Chimpanzees of Gombe.* Cambridge: Harvard University Press.

Goode, David. 1990. "On Understanding Without Words: Communication Between a Deaf-Blind Child and Her Parents." *Human Studies* 13:1–37.

———. 1992. "Who Is Bobby? Ideology and Method in the Discovery of a Down Syndrome Person's Competence." In Philip Ferguson, Dianne Ferguson, and Steven Taylor, eds., *Interpreting Disability: A Qualitative Reader,* 197–213. New York: Teachers College Press.

———. 1994. *A World Without Words: The Social Construction of Children Born Deaf and Blind.* Philadelphia: Temple University Press.

Goode, David, and Frances Waksler. 1990. "The Missing 'Who': Situational Identity and Fault-Finding with an Alingual Blind–Deaf Child." *Sociological Studies of Child Development* 3:203–223.

Gorelick, Sherry. 1991. "Contradictions of Feminist Methodology." *Gender and Society* 5:459–477.

Göring, Hermann. 1939. *The Political Testament of Hermann Göring.* Translated by H. W. Blood-Ryan. London: John Lang.

References

Gould, Steven Jay. 1991. *Wonderful Life: The Burgess Shale and the Nature of History*. Harmondsworth, England: Penguin.

Gouldner, Alvin. 1970. *The Coming Crisis of Western Sociology*. New York: Basic Books.

Gregory, Stanford, and Stephen Keto. 1991. "Creation of the 'Virtual Patient' in Medical Interaction: A Comparison of Doctor/Patient and Veterinarian/Client Relationships." Paper presented at the annual meeting of the American Sociological Association, Cincinnati. August.

Griffin, Donald. 1976. *The Question of Animal Awareness*. New York: Rockefeller University Press.

————. 1984. *Animal Thinking*. Cambridge: Harvard University Press.

————. 1992. *Animal Minds*. Chicago: University of Chicago Press.

Grunberger, Richard. 1971. *A Social History of the Third Reich*. London: Weidenfeld and Nicolson.

Gubrium, Jaber. 1986. "The Social Preservation of Mind: The Alzheimer's Disease Experience." *Symbolic Interaction* 9:37–51.

Hammersley, Martyn. 1990. *Reading Ethnographic Research*. London: Longman.

Haraway, Donna. 1989. *Primate Visions: Gender, Race, and Nature in the World of Modern Science*. New York: Routledge.

————. 1992. "The Promises of Monsters: A Regenerative Politics for Inappropriate/d Others." In Lawrence Grossberg, Cary Nelson, and Paula Treichler, eds., *Cultural Studies,* 295–337. New York: Routledge.

Harris, James. 1990. "Ethical Values of Individuals at Different Levels in the Organizational Hierarchy of a Single Firm." *Journal of Business Ethics* 9:741–750.

Hawley, Fred. 1993. "The Moral and Conceptual Universe of Cockfighters." *Society and Animals* 1:159–168.

Hayano, David. 1979. "Auto-Ethnography: Paradigms, Problems, and Prospects." *Human Organization* 38:99–104.

Hearne, Vicki. 1987. *Adam's Task*. New York: Knopf.

————. 1991. *Bandit*. New York: Harper Collins.

Hebb, D. O. 1946. "Emotion in Man and Animal: An Analysis of the Intuitive Processes of Recognition." *Psychological Review* 53:88–106.

Herzog, Harold. 1988. "The Moral Status of Mice." *American Psychologist* 43:473–474.

————. 1989. "Tangled Lives: Human Researchers and Animal Subjects." *Anthrozoös* 3:80–82.

————. 1993. "Human Morality and Animal Research." *American Scholar* 62:337–349.

Herzog, Harold, and Gordon Burghardt. 1988. "Attitudes Toward Animals: Origins and Diversity." In Andrew Rowan, ed., *Animals and People Sharing the World,* 75–94. Hanover, NH.: University Press of New England.

Herzog, Harold, and Shelley Galvin. 1992. "Animals, Archetypes, and Popular Culture: Tales from the Tabloid Press." *Anthrozoös* 5:77–92.

Herzog, Harold, Tamara Vore, and John New. 1989. "Conversations with Veterinary Students: Attitudes, Ethics, and Animals." *Anthrozoös* 2:181–188.

Herzstein, Robert. 1989. *The War That Hitler Won.* New York: Putnam.

Hewitt, John, and Randall Stokes. 1975. "Disclaimers." *American Sociological Review* 40:1–11.

Hickrod, Lucy, and Raymond Schmitt. 1982. "A Naturalistic Study of Interaction and Frame: The Pet as 'Family Member.'" *Urban Life* 11:55–77.

Higgins, Paul. 1992. *Making Disabilities: Exploring the Social Transformation of Human Variation.* Springfield, Ill.: Charles C. Thomas.

Hilberg, Raul. 1961. *The Destruction of the European Jews.* Chicago: Quadrangle.

Hilbert, Richard. 1994. "People Are Animals: Comment on Sanders and Arluke." *Sociological Quarterly* 35:533–536.

Hitler, Adolf. 1938. *Mein Kampf.* Munich: Franz Eher.

Hochschild, Arlie. 1983. *The Managed Heart: The Commercialization of Human Feeling.* Berkeley: University of California Press.

Hoelscher, H. 1949. "Tierschutz und Strafrecht." Doctoral dissertation, University of Heidelberg.

Holzner, Burkart. 1968. *Reality Construction in Society.* Cambridge, Mass.: Schenkman.

Hosey, Geoffrey, and Patricia Druck. 1987. "The Influence of Zoo Visitors on the Behaviour of Captive Primates." *Applied Animal Behaviour Science* 18:19–29.

Ingold, Tim, ed. 1988. *What Is an Animal?* London: Unwin Hyman.

Irving, David. 1989. *Göring.* New York: Morrow.

Johnson, John. 1975. *Doing Field Research.* New York: Free Press.

Jones, James H. 1981. *Bad Blood: The Tuskegee Syphilis Experiment.* New York: Free Press.

Jordan, James. 1975. "An Ambivalent Relationship: Dog and Human in the Folk Culture of the Rural South." *Appalachian Journal* 2:238–248.

Katcher, Aaron, and Alan Beck. 1991. "Animal Companions: More Companion Than Animal." In Michael Robinson and Lionel Tiger, eds., *Man and Beast Revisited,* 265–278. Washington, D.C.: Smithsonian Institution Press.

Katz, Jacob. 1986. *The Darker Side of Genius: Richard Wagner's Anti-Semitism.* Hanover, N.H.: University Press of New England.

Kaye, Kenneth. 1982. *The Mental and Social Life of Babies.* Chicago: University of Chicago Press.

Keller, Evelyn Fox. 1985. *Reflections on Gender and Science.* New Haven: Yale University Press.

Kellert, Stephen. 1978. "Attitudes and Characteristics of Hunters and Anti-hunters." *Transactions of the 43rd North American Wildlife and Natural Resources Conference* 43:412–423.

————. 1980. "Contemporary Values of Wildlife in American Society." In W. W. Shaw and E. H. Zube, eds., *Wildlife Values,* 31–39. Fort Collins, Colo.: U. S. Forest Service.

Kennedy, John S. 1992. *The New Anthropomorphism.* Cambridge: Cambridge University Press.

Kete, Kathleen. 1993. *The Beast in the Boudoir: Petkeeping in Nineteenth-Century Paris.* Berkeley: University of California Press.

Kielhofner, Gary. 1983. "'Teaching' Retarded Adults: Paradoxical Effects of a Pedagogical Enterprise." *Urban Life* 12:307–326.

Koehler, William. 1962. *The Koehler Method of Dog Training.* New York: Howell.

Koonz, Claudia. 1987. *Mothers in the Fatherland: Women, the Family, and Nazi Politics.* New York: St. Martin's.

Krieger, Susan. 1985. "Beyond Subjectivity: The Use of the Self in Social Science." *Qualitative Sociology* 8:309–324.

————. 1991. *Social Science and the Self.* New Brunswick, N.J.: Rutgers University Press.

Laidler, Keith. 1980. *The Talking Ape.* New York: Stein and Day.

Lane, Barbara, and Leila Rupp. 1978. *Nazi Ideology Before 1933.* Austin: University of Texas Press.

Langer, Walter. 1972. *The Mind of Adolf Hitler.* New York: Basic Books.

Lather, Patricia. 1991. *Getting Smart: Feminist Research and Pedagogy Within the Postmodern.* New York: Routledge.

Latour, Bruno. 1988. "Mixing Humans and Nonhumans Together: The Sociology of a Door-Closer." *Social Problems* 35:298–310.

Lawrence, Elizabeth. 1988. "Those Who Dislike Pets." *Anthrozoös* 1:147–148.

————. 1989. "Wild Birds: Therapeutic Encounters and Human Meanings." *Anthrozoös* 3:111–118.

————. 1990. "The Tamed Wild: Symbolic Bears in American Culture." In Ray Browne, Marshall Fishwick, and Kevin Browne, eds., *Dominant Sym-*

References　　　　　　　　　　　　　　　　　　　　　　　　　　　　　　*203*

bols in Popular Culture, 140–153. Bowling Green, Ohio: Bowling Green State University Popular Press.

Leach, Edmund. 1964. "Anthropological Aspects of Language: Animal Categories and Verbal Abuse." In E. H. Lenneberg, ed., *New Direction in the Study of Language*, 23–63. Cambridge: MIT Press.

Leasor, James. *Rudolf Hess.* 1962. London: George Allen Books.

Lenehan, Michael. 1986. "Four Ways to Walk a Dog." *The Atlantic Monthly* 257 (April): 35–48, 89–99.

Lerner, Richard. 1992. *Final Solutions: Biology, Prejudice, and Genocide.* University Park: Pennsylvania State University Press.

Lesy, Michael. 1987. *The Forbidden Zone.* New York: Farrar, Straus and Giroux.

Levin, Jack. 1994. "From Racism to Afrophobia." Unpublished manuscript, Department of Sociology, Northeastern University.

Lévi-Strauss, Claude. 1966. *The Savage Mind.* London: Weidenfeld and Nicolson.

Lifton, Robert. 1986. *The Nazi Doctors.* New York: Basic Books.

Lincoln, Y. S. and E. G. Guba. 1985. *Naturalistic Inquiry.* London: Sage Publications.

Lindesmith, Alfred, Anselm Strauss, and Norman Denzin. 1977. *Social Psychology.* 5th ed. New York: Holt, Rinehart and Winston.

Lorenz, Konrad. [1953] 1988. *Man Meets Dog.* New York: Penguin.

Lovejoy, E. O. 1936. *The Great Chain of Being.* New York: Harper Bros.

Lurie, Allison. 1982. *The Language of Clothing.* New York: Random House.

Lynch, Michael. 1983. "Accommodation Practices: Vernacular Treatment of Madness." *Social Problems* 31:152–164.

———. 1988. "Sacrifice and the Transformation of the Animal Body into a Scientific Object." *Social Studies of Science* 18:265–289.

Maltitz, Horst von. 1973. *The Evolution of Hitler's Germany.* New York: McGraw-Hill.

Mandell, Nancy. 1988. "The Least-Adult Role in Studying Children." *Journal of Contemporary Ethnography* 16:433–468.

Manvell, Roger, and Heinrich Fraenkel. 1971. *Hess.* London: George Allen and Unwin.

Maple, Terry. 1995. "Toward a Responsible Zoo Agenda." In Bryan Norton et al., eds., *Ethics on the Ark: Zoos, Animal Welfare, and Wildlife Conservation,* 20–30. Washington, D.C.: Smithsonian Institution Press.

McConnell, Patricia. 1991. "Lessons from Animal Trainers: The Effect of Acoustic Structure on an Animal's Response." In P.P.G. Bateson and Peter Klopfer, eds., *Perspectives on Ethology* 9:165–187. New York: Plenum.

References

McGovern, James. 1968. *Martin Bormann.* New York: Morrow.

McTear, Michael. 1985. *Children's Conversation.* New York: Basil Blackwell.

Mead, George Herbert. [1934] 1964. *On Social Psychology.* Edited by Anselm Strauss. Chicago: University of Chicago Press.

Meddin, Jay. 1979. "Chimpanzees, Symbols, and the Reflective Self." *Social Psychology Quarterly* 42:99–109.

Melena, E. 1877. *Gemma, oder Tugend und Laster.* Munich: G. Franz.

Menzell, E. W. and S. Halperin. 1975. "Purposive Behavior as a Basis for Objective Communication Between Chimpanzees." *Science* 229:652–654.

Meyer, Helmut. 1975. *Der Mensch und das Tier: Anthropologische und Kulturoziologishe Aspekte.* Munich: Heinz Moos.

———. 1993. "Response to Arluke and Sax." *Anthrozoös* 6:88–90.

Miale, Florence, and Michael Selzer. 1975. *The Nuremberg Mind.* New York: Quadrangle.

Midgley, Mary. 1988. "Beasts, Brutes and Monsters." In Tim Ingold, ed., *What Is an Animal?* 35–46. London: Unwin Hyman.

———. 1989. "Motivation of Scientists." *Anthrozoös* 3:85–86.

Mies, Maria. 1983. "Towards a Methodology for Feminist Research." In Gloria Bowles and Renate Klein, eds., *Theories in Women's Studies,* 117–139. Boston: Routledge and Kegan Paul.

Milgram, Stanley. 1974. *Obedience to Authority.* New York: Harper and Row.

Miller, Marc, and John Van Maanen. 1982. "Getting Into Fishing: Observations on the Social Identities of New England Fishermen." *Urban Life* 11:38–54.

Mills, C. Wright. 1940. "Situated Actions and Vocabularies of Motive." *American Sociological Review* 5:904–913.

———. 1959. *The Sociological Imagination.* New York: Oxford University Press.

Mosse, George. 1966. *Nazi Culture: Intellectual, Cultural, and Social Life in the Third Reich.* Translated by Salvator Attanasio et al. New York: Grosset & Dunlap.

Mullan, Bob, and Garry Marvin. 1987. *Zoo Culture.* London: Weidenfeld and Nicolson.

Myrdal, Gunnar. 1944. *An American Dilemma.* New York: Harper Bros.

Nash, Jeffrey. 1989. "What's in a Face? The Social Character of the English Bulldog." *Qualitative Sociology* 12:357–370.

Nash, Jeffrey, and Anne Sutherland. 1991. "The Moral Elevation of Animals: The Case of *Gorillas in the Mist.*" *International Journal of Politics, Culture, and Society* 5:111–126.

References

Neff, Roland. 1989. *Der Streit um den Wissenschaftlichen Tierversuch in der Schweiz des 19 Jahrhunderts.* Basel: Schwabe.

Nelson, James. 1989. "Symbol and Sensibility." *Anthrozoös* 3:86–88.

Padfield, Peter. 1984. *Dönitz: The Last Führer.* New York: Harper and Row.

Palmer, C. Eddie. 1985. "Keepers of the King's Deer: Game Wardens and the Enforcement of Fish and Wildlife Law." In Clifton Bryant, Donald Shoemaker, James Skipper, Jr., and William Snizek, eds., *The Rural Work Force: Nonagricultural Occupations in America,* 111–137. South Hadley, Mass.: Bergin and Garvey.

Patterson, Francine, and Eugene Linden. 1981. *The Education of Koko.* New York: Holt, Rinehart and Winston.

Payne, Robert. 1960. *The Life and Death of Adolf Hitler.* New York: Praeger.

Perez, Berta. 1986. "Midwesterners' Perceptions of and Attitudes Towards Pets." *Central Issues in Anthropology* 6:13–24.

Perin, Constance. 1981. "Dogs as Symbols in Human Development." In Bruce Fogle, ed., *Interrelations Between People and Pets,* 68–88. Springfield, Ill.: Charles C. Thomas.

Peukert, Detlev. 1987. *Inside Nazi Germany: Conformity, Opposition, and Racism in Everyday Life.* New Haven: Yale University Press.

Phillips, Mary. 1993. "Savages, Drunks, and Lab Animals: The Researcher's Perception of Pain." *Society and Animals* 1:61–81.

Piaget, Jean. 1926. *The Language and Thought of the Child.* London: K. Paul, Trench, Trubner.

Pike, Kenneth. 1954. *Language in Relation to a Unified Theory of the Structure of Human Behavior,* Part 1. The Hague: Mouton.

Pitt, David. 1972. *Using Historical Sources in Anthropology and Sociology.* New York: Holt, Rinehart and Winston.

Plant, Judith, ed. 1989. *Healing the World: The Promise of Ecofeminism.* Philadelphia: New Society.

Pollner, Melvin, and David Goode. 1990. "Ethnomethodology and Person-Centering Practices." *Person-Centered Review* 5:203–220.

Pollner, Melvin, and Lynn McDonald-Wikler. 1985. "The Social Construction of Unreality: A Case of a Family's Attribution of Competence to a Severely Retarded Child." *Family Process* 24:241–254.

Posner, Gerald, and John Ware. 1986. *Mengele.* New York: McGraw-Hill.

Premack, David, and Guy Woodruff. 1978. "Does the Chimpanzee Have a Theory of Mind?" *Behavioral and Brain Science* 1:515–526.

Proctor, Robert. 1988. *Racial Hygiene.* Cambridge: Harvard University Press.

Radde, Glenn. 1991. Personal communication.

Rasmussen, Jeffrey, D. W. Rajecki, and H. D. Craft. 1993. "Human Perceptions of Animal Mentality: Ascriptions of Thinking." *Journal of Comparative Psychology* 107:283–290.

Rhodes, James. 1980. *The Hitler Movement: A Modern Millenarian Movement.* Stanford, Calif.: Hoover Institution Press.

Ristau, Carolyn, ed. 1991. *Cognitive Ethology: The Minds of Other Animals.* Hillsdale, N.J.: Lawrence Erlbaum.

Robbins, Douglas, Clinton Sanders, and Spencer Cahill. 1991. "Dogs and Their People: Pet Facilitated Interaction in a Public Setting." *Journal of Contemporary Ethnography* 20:3–25.

Rochberg-Halton, Eugene. 1985. "Life in the Treehouse: Pet Therapy as Family Metaphor and Self-Dialogue." In Marvin Sussman, ed., *Pets and the Family,* 175–190. New York: Haworth.

Rollin, Bernard. 1989. "Animals in Experimentation: Utilitarian Objects, Pets, or Moral Objects." *Anthrozoös* 3:88–90.

———. 1990. *The Unheeded Cry: Animal Consciousness, Animal Pain, and Science.* New York: Oxford University Press.

Rosenberg, Alfred. 1935. *Der Mythus des 20 Jahrhunderts.* Munich: Hoheneichen-Verlag.

Ross, John, and Barbara McKinney. 1992. *Dog Talk.* New York: St. Martin's.

Rowan, Andrew, ed. 1986. *Dog Aggression and the Pit Bull Terrier.* North Grafton, Mass.: Tufts School of Veterinary Medicine, Workshop Proceedings, July.

———. 1991. "The Human–Animal Interface: Chasm or Continuum?" In Michael Robinson and Lionel Tiger, eds., *Man and Beast Revisited,* 279–290. Washington, D.C.: Smithsonian Institution Press.

Russell, Constance. 1995. "The Social Construction of Orangutans: An Ecotourist Experience." *Society and Animals* 3:151–170.

Sacks, Harvey, Emmanuel Schegloff, and Gail Jefferson. 1974. "A Simplest Systematics for the Organization of Turn-Taking for Conversation." *Language* 50:696–735.

Sanders, Clinton. 1990a. "Excusing Tactics: Social Responses to the Public Misbehavior of Companion Animals." *Anthrozoös* 4:82–90.

———. 1990b. "The Animal Other: Self Definition, Social Identity, and Companion Animals." In Gerald Gorn, Richard Pollay, and Marvin Goldberg, eds., *Advances in Consumer Research* 17:662–668. Provo, Utah: Association for Consumer Research.

References 207

————. 1993. "Understanding Dogs: Caretakers' Attributions of Mindedness in Canine–Human Relationships." *Journal of Contemporary Ethnography* 22:205–226.

Sax, Boria. 1990. *The Frog King: On Legends, Fables, Fairy Tales, and Anecdotes of Animals.* New York: Pace University Press.

————. N.d. "The Zoo as an Experiment in Utopia," Unpublished manuscript.

Schleifer, Harriet. 1985 . "Images of Death and Life: Food Animal Production and the Vegetarian Option." In Peter Singer, ed., *In Defense of Animals,* 63–74. New York: Harper and Row.

Schopenhauer, Arthur. 1903. *The Basis of Morality.* Translated by A. B. Bullock. London: Swann, Sonnenschein.

Schröder, Beate. 1976. "Das Tierschutzgesetz vom 24:11.1933." Med. vet. dissertation, Berlin.

Schutz, Alfred. 1962. *Collected Papers.* Vol. 1, *The Problem of Social Reality.* The Hague: Nijhoff.

————. 1970. *On Phenomenology and Social Relations.* Chicago: University of Chicago Press.

Scott, Marvin, and Stanford Lyman. 1968. "Accounts." *American Sociological Review* 33:46–62.

Sebeok, Thomas. 1981. *The Play of Musement.* Bloomington: Indiana University Press.

Selzer, Michael. 1972. *"Kike!" A Documentary History of Anti-Semitism in America.* New York: World Publishers.

Serpe, Richard. 1987. "Stability and Change in Self: A Structural Symbolic Interactionist Explanation." *Social Psychology Quarterly* 50:44–55.

Serpell, James. 1986. *In the Company of Animals.* Oxford: Basil Blackwell.

————. 1995. Personal communication.

Shaffir, William, Robert Stebbins, and Allan Turowetz, eds. 1980. *Fieldwork Experience: Qualitative Approaches to Social Research.* New York: St. Martin's.

Shanklin, Eugenia. 1985. "Sustenance and Symbol: Anthropological Studies of Domesticated Animals." *Annual Review of Anthropology* 14:375–403.

Shapiro, Kenneth. 1989. "The Death of the Animal: Ontological Vulnerability." *Between the Species* 5:183–193.

————. 1990a. "Animal Rights Versus Humanism: The Charge of Speciesism." *Journal of Humanistic Psychology* 30:9–37.

————. 1990b. "Understanding Dogs Through Kinesthetic Empathy, Social Construction, and History." *Anthrozoös* 3:184–195.

Sheets-Johnstone, Maxine. 1992. "The Possibility of an Evolutionary Semantics." *Between the Species* 8:88–94.

Shirer, William L. 1960. *The Rise and Fall of the Third Reich*. New York: Simon & Schuster.

Sklar, Dusty. 1977. *Gods and Beasts: The Nazis and the Occult*. New York: T.Y. Crowell.

Smith, Allen, III, and Sherryl Kleinman. 1989. "Managing Emotions in Medical School: Students' Contacts with the Living and the Dead." *Social Psychology Quarterly* 52:56–68.

Smith, Carolyn, and William Kornblum, eds. 1989. *In the Field: Readings on the Field Research Experience*. New York: Praeger.

Sontag, Susan. 1977. *On Photography*. New York: Farrar, Straus & Giroux.

Speer, Albert. 1970. *Inside the Third Reich*. New York: Macmillan.

Sperling, Susan. 1988. *Animal Liberators: Research and Morality*. Berkeley: University of California Press.

Staff, Ilse, ed. 1964. *Justiz im Dritten Reich: Eine Dokumentation*. Frankfort: Fischer Bucherei.

Staudinger, Hans. 1981. *The Inner Nazi*. Baton Rouge: Louisiana State University Press.

Stebbins, Sarah. 1993. "Anthropomorphism." *Philosophical Studies* 69:113–122.

Stone, Norman. 1980. *Hitler*. Boston: Little, Brown.

Strum, Shirley. 1987. *Almost Human*. London: Elm Tree.

Tabor, Roger. 1983. *The Wildlife of the Domestic Cat*. London: Arrow Books.

Tambiah, Stanley. 1969. "Animals are Good to Think and Good to Prohibit." *Ethnology* 8:423–459.

Tannen, Deborah, and Cynthia Wallat. 1983. "Doctor/Mother/Child Communication: Linguistic Analysis of a Pediatric Interaction." In Sue Fisher and Alexandra D. Todd, eds., *The Social Organization of Doctor–Patient Communication*, 203–219. Washington, D.C.: Center for Applied Linguistics.

Tanner, Nancy. 1981. *On Becoming Human*. Cambridge: Cambridge University Press.

Terrace, Herbert. 1987. "Thoughts Without Words." In Colin Blakemore and Susan Greenfield, eds., *Mindwaves: Thoughts on Intelligence, Identity, and Consciousness*, 123–137. New York: Basil Blackwell.

Tester, Keith. 1991. *Animals and Society*. London: Routledge.

Thomas, Bill. 1985. *Talking with the Animals*. New York: Morrow.

Thomas, Elizabeth Marshall. 1993. *The Hidden Life of Dogs*. New York: Houghton Mifflin.

References   209

Thomas, Keith. 1983. *Man and the Natural World: Changing Attitudes in England, 1500–1800.* London: Allen Lane.

Toland, John. 1976. *Adolf Hitler.* Garden City, N.Y.: Doubleday.

Toth, Jennifer. 1993. *The Mole People.* Chicago: Chicago Review Press.

Trohler, Ulrich, and Andreas-Holger Maehle. 1987. "Anti-Vivisection in Nineteenth-Century Germany: Motives and Methods." In Nicolaas A. Rupke, ed., *Vivisection in Historical Perspective,* 149–187. New York: Croom Helm.

Tuan, Yi-Fu. 1984. *Dominance and Affection: The Making of Pets.* New Haven: Yale University Press.

Turkle, Sherry. 1984. *The Second Self.* New York: Simon & Schuster.

U.S. News and World Report. 1987. "The Most Dangerous Dog in America," April 20, p. 24.

Veevers, Jean. 1985. "The Social Meaning of Pets: Alternative Roles for Companion Animals." In Marvin Sussman, ed., *Pets and the Family,* 11–30. New York: Haworth.

Viereck, Peter. 1965. *Metapolitics: The Roots of the Nazi Mind.* New York: Capricorn.

Voith, Victoria. 1983. "Animal Behavior Problems: An Overview." In Aaron Katcher and Alan Beck, eds., *New Perspectives on Our Lives with Companion Animals,* 181–187. Philadelphia: University of Pennsylvania Press.

Wagner, Richard. 1888a. "Heldentum and Christenheit." In *Gesammelte Schriften und Dichtungen* 10:275–285. Leipzig: G.W. Fritsch.

———. 1888b. "Offenes Schreiben an Ernst von Weber." In *Gesammelte Schriften und Dichtungen* 10:195–210. Leipzig: G.W. Fritsch.

———. 1987. *Selected Letters of Richard Wagner.* Edited and translated by Stewart Spencer and Barry Millington. New York: Norton.

Waite, Robert. 1977. *The Psychopathic God: Adolf Hitler.* New York: Basic Books.

Weinstein, Fred. 1980. *The Dynamics of Nazism: Leadership, Ideology, and the Holocaust.* New York: Academic Press.

Wemelsfelder, Françoise. 1993. *Animal Boredom: Towards an Empirical Approach to Animal Subjectivity.* Utrecht, Netherlands: Elinkwijk.

West, Candace, and Don Zimmerman. 1977. "Women's Place in Everyday Talk: Reflections on Parent–Child Interaction." *Social Problems* 24: 521–529.

Whyte, William F. 1955. *Street Corner Society.* Chicago: University of Chicago Press.

Wieder, D. Lawrence. 1980. "Behavioristic Operationalism and the Life–World: Chimpanzees and Chimpanzee Researchers in Face-to-Face Interaction." *Sociological Inquiry* 50:75–103.

Wilder, Hugh. 1990. "Interpretive Cognitive Ethology." In Marc Bekoff and Dale Jamieson, eds., *Interpretation and Explanation in the Study of Animal Behavior* 1:344–368. Boulder, Colo.: Westview.

Willis, Roy. 1974. *Man and Beast*. London: Hart-Davis, MacGibbon.

———ed. 1990. *Signifying Animals*. London: Unwin Hyman.

Wittgenstein, Ludwig. 1958. *Philosophical Investigations*. Translated by G.E.M. Anscombe. 2d ed. Oxford: Basil Blackwell.

Woltmann, Ludwig. 1936. *Politische Anthropologie: Woltmann's Werke*, Vol. I. Leipzig: Dorner.

Woodward, C. Vann. 1966. *The Strange Career of Jim Crow*. New York: Oxford University Press.

Wuttke-Groneberg, W. 1980. *Medizin im Nationalsozialismus*. Tübingen: Schwabische Verlaggesellschaft.

Zihlman, Adrienne. 1978. "Women and Evolution, Part II: Subsistence and Social Organization Among Early Hominids." *Signs* 4:4–20.

Zöllner, Friedrich. 1885. *Über den Wissenschaftlichen Missbrauch der Vivisektion*. Leipzig: Gustav Fock.

References

index

"action reproduction," 48
"afrophobia," 186
ageism, 172–173, 189
Alzheimer's disease, 63, 70
ambivalence. *See* animals
American Dilemma, An (Myrdal),
189–190
American Sign Language, 47
American Werewolf in London, 181
androcentrism, 42. *See also* anthropocentrism
animal experimentation, 20, 22, 23,
24–25, 28–29, 34, 39–40, 173–174,
178–179; in primate labs, 24, 50–51,
107–131. *See also* Nazi Germany
animal shelter workers, 82–106; and
adoption, 92–93; anger of, at pet
owners, 96–99; and avoidance of
euthanasia, 93–95; dilemmas of,
84–86; emotion-management by,
86–106; euthanasia as problem for,
37, 84–106; focus on animals' feelings by, 89–93; and mascots, 89;
redefinition of animals by, 86–89,
89–93; relationships of, with
outsiders, 99–101
animals: addiction to, 122; ambivalence
about, 4–5, 28, 54, 105–106, 167–186;
anthropological study of, 3; "bad,"
169–170, 175–186; as "behavioristic
machines," 49, 74; communication
with, 47–50, 67–68, 128; "good,"
170–175; liminal, 86–89; minds of,

42–52, 65–66, 67, 78–81; moral elevation of, 115–122, 137–147; in Nazi
Germany, 132–166; objectification
of, 109–115, 154; and object–pet dichotomy, 105–106; "personhood" of,
44, 65–66; sentience of, 51–52; social
constructions of, 10–18, 130–131,
167–186, 191; sociological study of,
2–3; as symbols, 3, 186; as tools, 170,
173–175; as "virtual pets," 86–88;
wild versus tame, 10, 14–17, 173
animal's perspective, 41–57, 61–81,
89–93, 103
anthropocentrism, 2, 42, 49, 145–146
anthropomorphism, 14, 47, 49, 52; critical, 80–81
anti-Semitism, 136, 144, 153–166,
179–180
apes, 47, 134, 145, 176, 182
Aristotle, 168
Arluke, Arnold, 19, 20, 22, 23, 24–25,
28, 32, 34–36, 37, 39, 173, 174
atavistic theory, 176
auto-ethnography, 29–30. *See also*
ethnography

Baby Fae case, 177
Baker, Steve, 188
Balinese, 3, 108
Barnard, Neal, 135
"because-motives," 62
Beck, Alan, 66, 67–68
Becker, Howard, 24, 38, 39

Index